Contents

What's Great About This Book

Centers are a wonderful, fun way for students to practice important skills. The 13 centers in this book are self-contained and portable. Students may work at a desk, table, or even on the floor. Once you've made the centers, they're ready to use any time.

What's in This Book

The teacher direction page includes how to make the center and a description of the student task.

Full-color materials needed for the center

Reproducible activity sheets

Self-checking answer keys

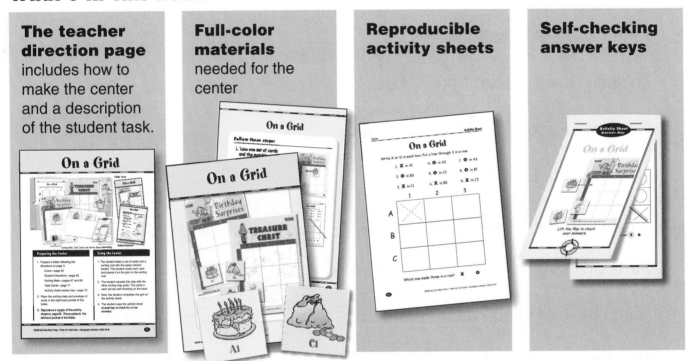

How to Use the Centers

The centers are intended for skill practice, not to introduce skills. It is important to model the use of each center before students do the task independently.

Questions to Consider:

- Will students select a center, or will you assign the centers?
- Will there be a specific block of time for centers, or will the centers be used throughout the day?
- Where will you place the centers for easy access by students?
- What procedure will students use when they need help with the center tasks?
- Where will students store completed work?
- How will you track the tasks and centers completed by each student?

Making a File Folder Center

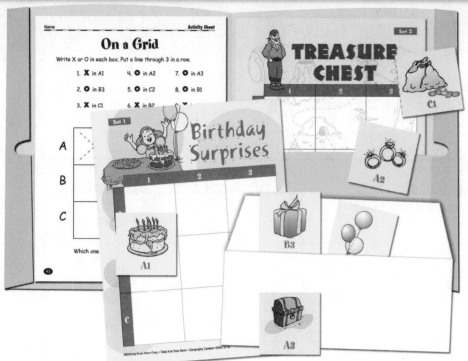

> Folder centers are easily stored in a box or file crate. Students take a folder to their desks to complete the task.

Materials

- folder with pockets
- envelopes
- marking pens and pencils
- scissors
- stapler
- two-sided tape

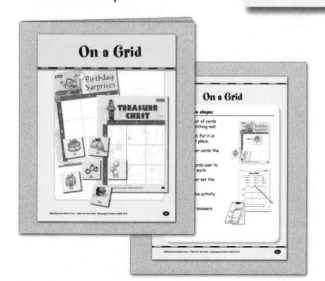

Steps to Follow

1. Laminate the cover. Tape it to the front of the folder.

2. Laminate the student direction page. Tape it to the back of the folder.

3. Laminate the self-checking answer key for each center. Cut the page in half. Staple the cover on top of the answer key. Place the answer key in the left-hand pocket.

4. Place activity sheets, writing paper, and any other supplies in the left-hand pocket.

5. Laminate the task cards. Place each set of task cards in an envelope. Place the labeled envelopes in the right-hand pocket.

6. If needed for the center, tape the sorting mat together. Laminate it and fold in half before placing it in the right-hand pocket of the folder.

Center Checklist

Student Names

Centers

Centers										
At the Zoo										
Looking Down										
Compass Rose										
North, South, East, West										
On a Grid										
Parts of a Map										
Name It										
Map Keys										
Our World										
North America										
United States of America										
Make a Map										
Read a Map										

At the Zoo

Folder Cover

Sorting Mat, Task Cards, and Activity Sheet Answer Key

Student Directions

Preparing the Center

1. Prepare a folder following the directions on page 3.

    Cover—page 7

    Student Directions—page 9

    Sorting Mat—pages 11 and 13

    Task Cards—page 15

    Activity Sheet Answer Key—page 17

2. Place the sorting mat and the envelope of cards in the right-hand pocket of the folder.

3. Reproduce a supply of the activity sheet on page 6. Place copies in the left-hand pocket of the folder.

Using the Center

1. The student takes the sorting mat, the envelope of task cards, and an activity sheet.

2. The student reads each card and places it in the correct box on the sorting mat. The cards are self-checking on the back.

3. Next, the student answers the questions on the activity sheet by circling *yes* or *no*.

4. The student uses the activity sheet answer key to check his or her answers.

At the Zoo

Look at the animals on the mat.

Circle **yes** or **no** to answer the question.

1 Is the monkey **under** the tree?   yes   no

2 Is the dog **by** the pool?   yes   no

3 Is the bird **over** the house?   yes   no

4 Is the turtle **under** the tree?   yes   no

5 Is the giraffe **on** the hill?   yes   no

6 Is the elephant **in** the lake?   yes   no

7 Is the seal **in** the tree?   yes   no

8 Is the bear **behind** the fence?   yes   no

At the Zoo

At the Zoo

Follow these steps:

1. Take the mat and the cards.

2. Read a card. Put it in the correct place.

   Do the other cards the same way.

3. Turn the cards over to check your work.

4. Complete the activity sheet.

   Check your answers.

AT THE ZOO

Map Key

pool

tree

fence

lake

hill

house

in the tree

in the pool

over the pool

by the pool

behind the fence

under the tree

in the lake

on the hill

in the house

At the Zoo

©2005 by Evan-Moor Corp.
EMC 3716

At the Zoo

©2005 by Evan-Moor Corp.
EMC 3716

At the Zoo

©2005 by Evan-Moor Corp. • EMC
3716

At the Zoo

©2005 by Evan-Moor Corp.
EMC 3716

At the Zoo

©2005 by Evan-Moor Corp.
EMC 3716

At the Zoo

©2005 by Evan-Moor Corp.
EMC 3716

At the Zoo

©2005 by Evan-Moor Corp.
EMC 3716

At the Zoo

©2005 by Evan-Moor Corp.
EMC 3716

At the Zoo

©2005 by Evan-Moor Corp.
EMC 3716

At the Zoo

1. no
2. yes
3. no
4. yes
5. yes
6. no
7. no
8. yes

At the Zoo

Lift the flap to check
your answers.

At the Zoo

©2005 by Evan-Moor Corp. • EMC 3716

At the Zoo

©2005 by Evan-Moor Corp. • EMC 3716

Looking Down

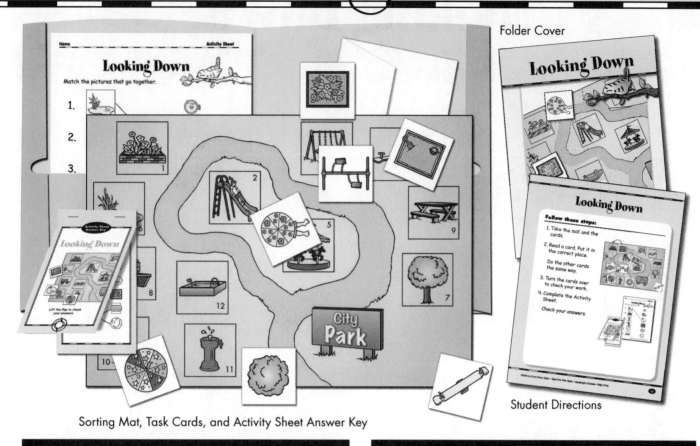

Folder Cover

Student Directions

Sorting Mat, Task Cards, and Activity Sheet Answer Key

Preparing the Center

1. Prepare a folder following the directions on page 3.

   Cover—page 21

   Student Directions—page 23

   Sorting Mat—pages 25 and 27

   Task Cards—page 29

   Activity Sheet Answer Key—page 31

2. Place the sorting mat and the envelope of cards in the right-hand pocket of the folder.

3. Reproduce a supply of the activity sheet on page 20. Place copies in the left-hand pocket of the folder.

Using the Center

1. The student takes the sorting mat, the envelope of task cards, and an activity sheet.

2. The student looks at each card and places it on top of the matching picture. The cards are self-checking on the back.

3. Next, the student completes the activity sheet by drawing a line to match the two views of the same item.

4. The student uses the activity sheet answer key to check his or her answers.

Looking Down

Match the pictures that go together.

1.

2.

3.

4.

5.

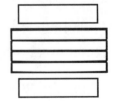

6.

Looking Down

Looking Down

Follow these steps:

1. Take the mat and the cards.

2. Read a card. Put it in the correct place.

   Do the other cards the same way.

3. Turn the cards over to check your work.

4. Complete the activity sheet.

   Check your answers.

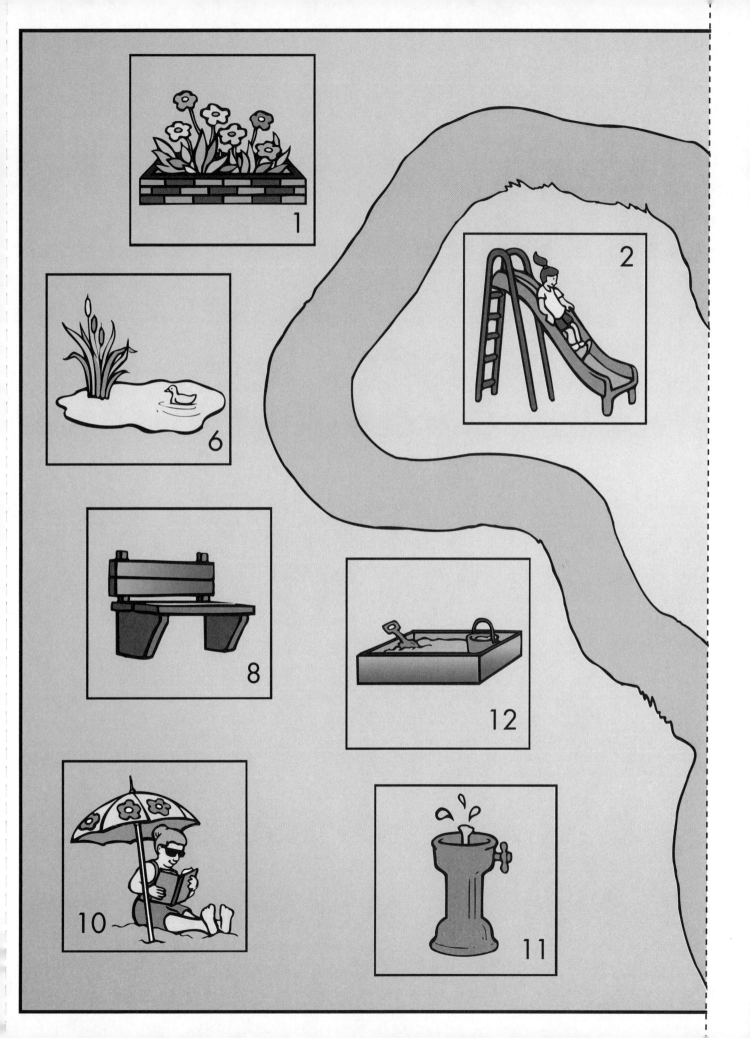

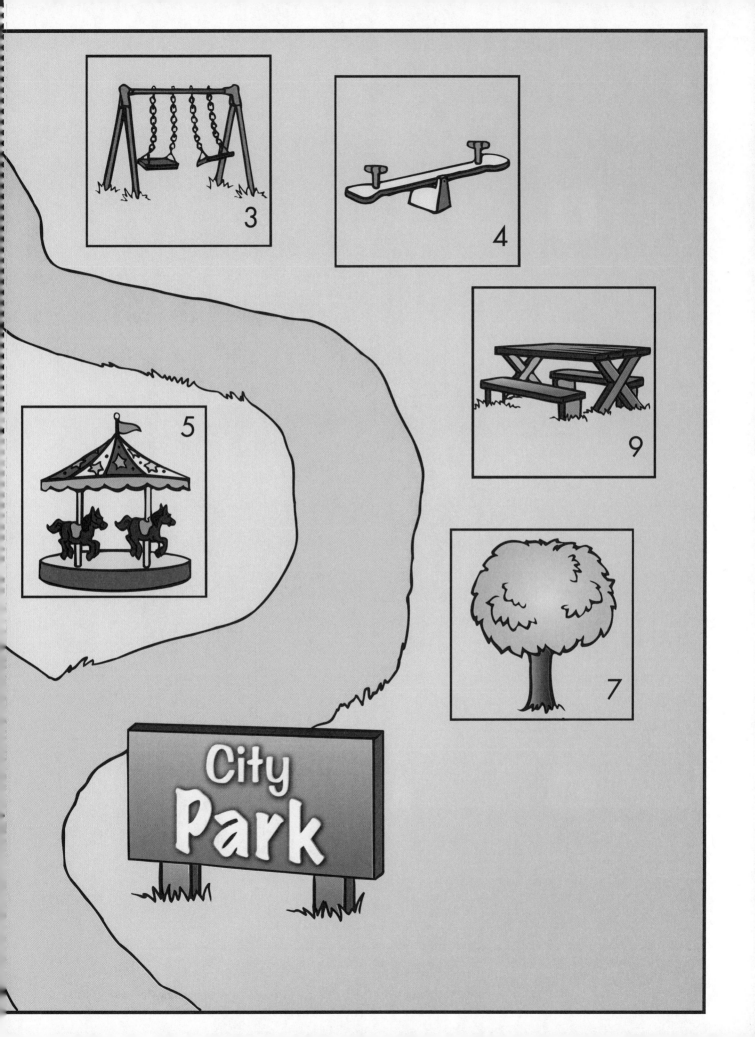

8

Looking Down

©2005 by Evan-Moor Corp.
EMC 3716

6

Looking Down

©2005 by Evan-Moor Corp.
EMC 3716

1

Looking Down

©2005 by Evan-Moor Corp.
EMC 3716

12

Looking Down

©2005 by Evan-Moor Corp.
EMC 3716

11

Looking Down

©2005 by Evan-Moor Corp.
EMC 3716

10

Looking Down

©2005 by Evan-Moor Corp.
EMC 3716

3

Looking Down

©2005 by Evan-Moor Corp.
EMC 3716

5

Looking Down

©2005 by Evan-Moor Corp.
EMC 3716

2

Looking Down

©2005 by Evan-Moor Corp.
EMC 3716

7

Looking Down

©2005 by Evan-Moor Corp.
EMC 3716

9

Looking Down

©2005 by Evan-Moor Corp.
EMC 3716

4

Looking Down

©2005 by Evan-Moor Corp.
EMC 3716

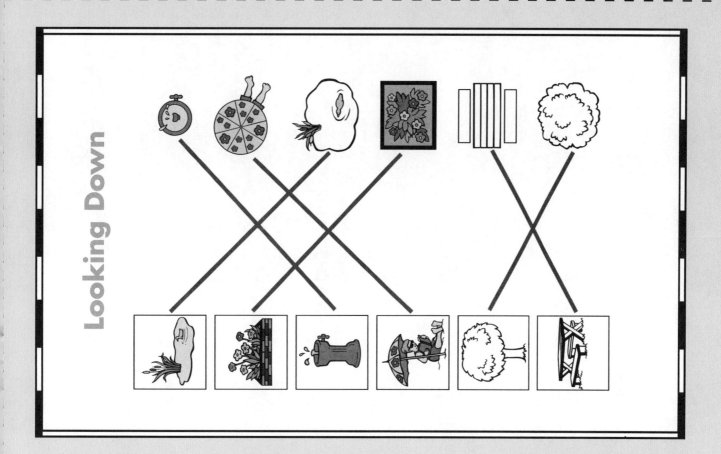

Looking Down

©2005 by Evan-Moor Corp. • EMC 3716

Looking Down

©2005 by Evan-Moor Corp. • EMC 3716

Compass Rose

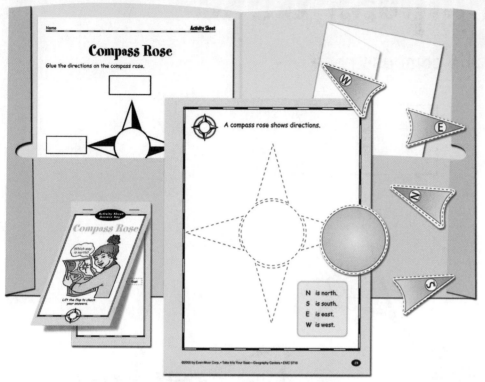

Folder Cover

Sorting Mat, Puzzle Pieces, and Activity Sheet Answer Key

Student Directions

Preparing the Center

1. Prepare a folder following the directions on page 3.

   Cover—page 35

   Student Directions—page 37

   Sorting Mat—page 39

   Puzzle Pieces—page 41

   Activity Sheet Answer Key—page 43

2. Place the sorting mat and the envelope of puzzle pieces in the right-hand pocket of the folder.

3. Reproduce a supply of the activity sheet on page 34. Place copies in the left-hand pocket of the folder.

Using the Center

1. The student takes the sorting mat, the envelope of puzzle pieces, and an activity sheet.

2. The student removes the puzzle pieces from the envelope and places them in the correct location on the mat.

3. Next, the student completes the activity sheet by cutting out the direction labels and correctly gluing them on the compass rose.

4. The student uses the activity sheet answer key to check his or her answers.

Compass Rose

Glue the directions on the compass rose.

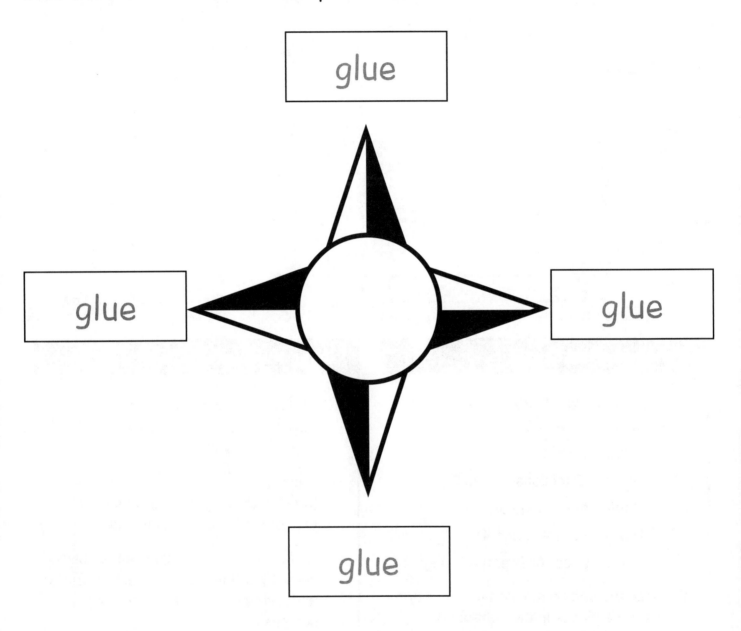

glue

glue glue

glue

| North | South | East | West |

Compass Rose

Compass Rose

Follow these steps:

1. Take the puzzle pieces and the mat.

2. Place the puzzle pieces in the correct places on the mat.

3. Turn the pieces over to check your work.

4. Complete the activity sheet.

   Check your answers.

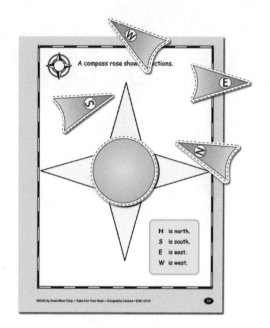

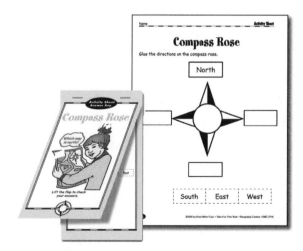

A compass rose shows directions.

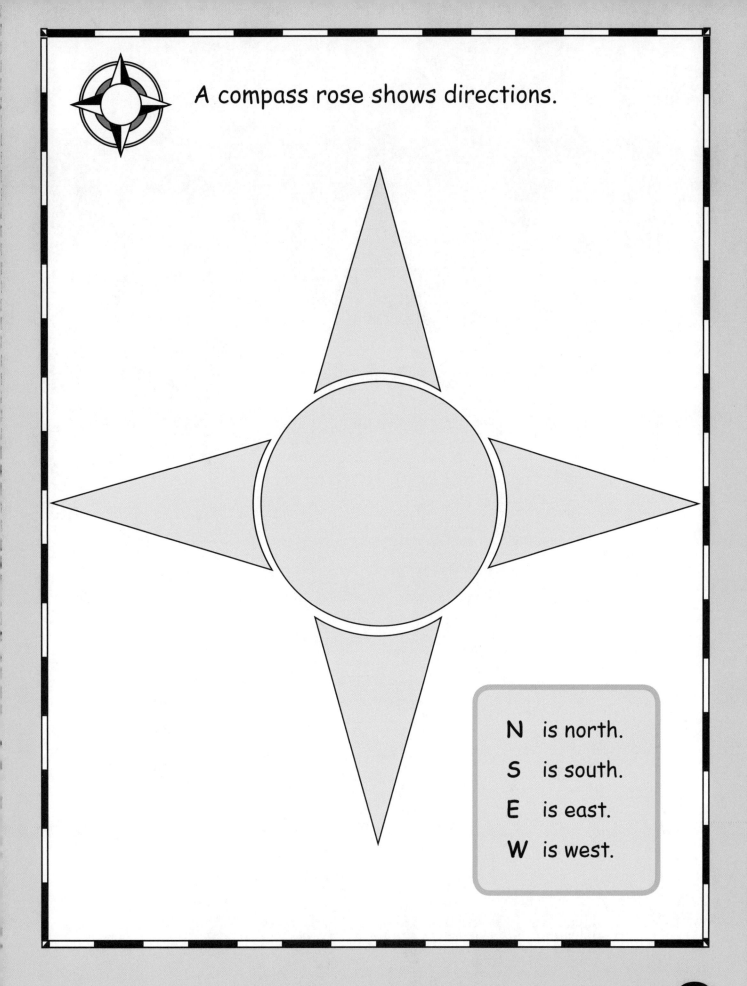

N is north.
S is south.
E is east.
W is west.

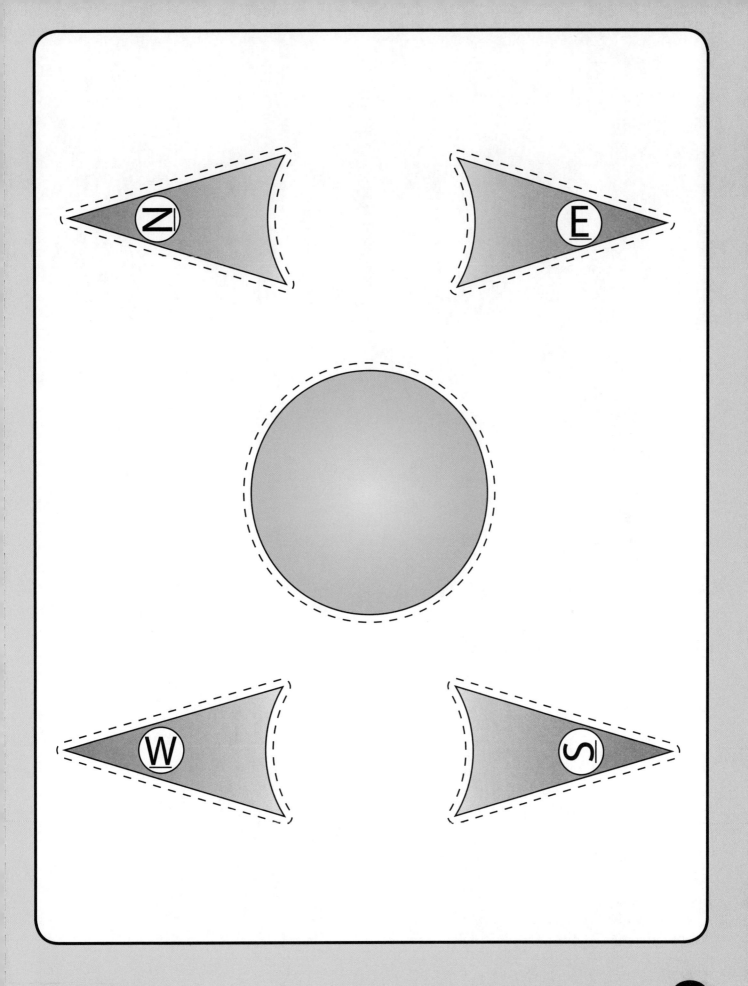

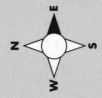

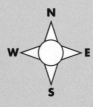

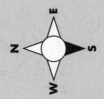

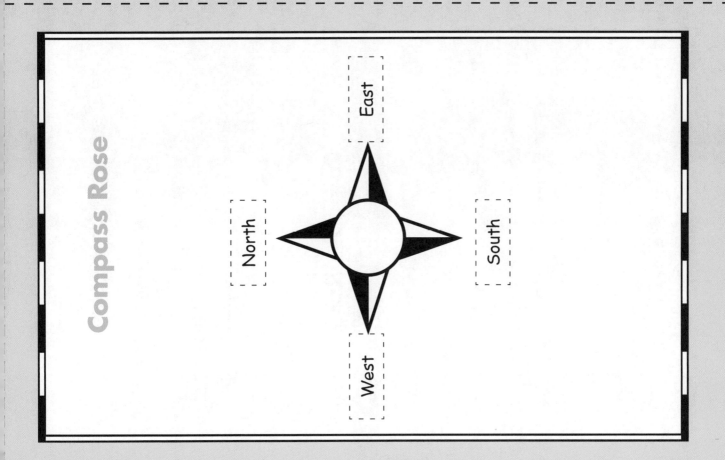

Compass Rose

Which way is north?

Lift the flap to check your answers.

Compass Rose

©2005 by Evan-Moor Corp. • EMC 3716

Compass Rose

©2005 by Evan-Moor Corp. • EMC 3716

North, South, East, West

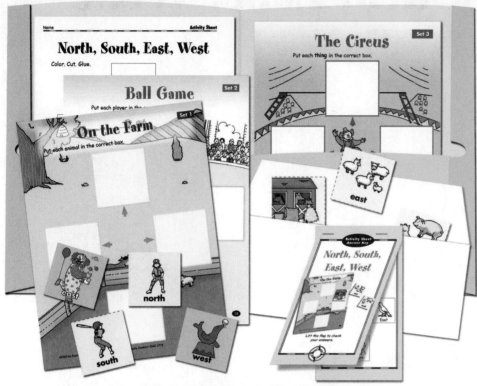

Folder Cover

Sorting Mats, Task Cards, and Activity Sheet Answer Key

Student Directions

Preparing the Center

1. Prepare a folder following the directions on page 3.

    Cover—page 47

    Student Directions—page 49

    Sorting Mats—pages 51–55

    Task Cards—page 57

    Activity Sheet Answer Key—page 59

2. Place the sorting mats and the envelopes of cards in the right-hand pocket of the folder.

3. Reproduce a supply of the activity sheet on page 46. Place copies in the left-hand pocket of the folder.

Using the Center

1. The student selects one set of cards, the matching mat, and an activity sheet.

2. The student reads each card and then places it in the correct location on the sorting mat.

3. The student repeats this step with the other two sets of cards. The cards are self-checking on the back.

4. Finally, the student completes the activity sheet by cutting out the pictures and gluing them in the correct locations.

5. The student uses the activity sheet answer key to check his or her answers.

North, South, East, West

Color. Cut. Glue.

glue

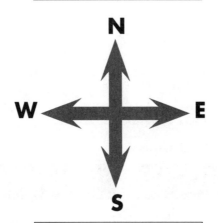

glue

glue

glue

north

south

east

west

North, South, East, West

North, South, East, West

Follow these steps:

1. Take one set of cards and the matching mat.

2. Read a card. Put it in the correct place.

   Do the other cards the same way.

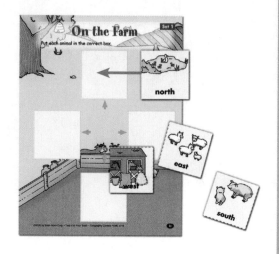

3. Turn the cards over to check your work.

4. Do the other sets the same way.

5. Complete the activity sheet.

   Check your answers.

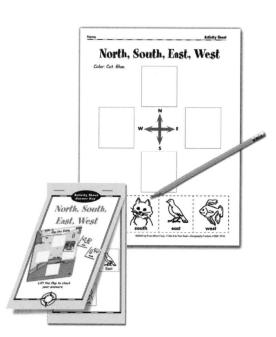

On the Farm

Set 1

Put each animal in the correct box.

North, South, East, West

©2005 by Evan-Moor Corp. • EMC 3716

Ball Game

Put each player in the correct box.

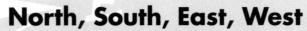

North, South, East, West

©2005 by Evan-Moor Corp. • EMC 3716

The Circus

Put each thing in the correct box.

North, South, East, West

©2005 by Evan-Moor Corp. • EMC 3716

 **east**	**north**	**north**
west	**west**	**south**
north	**south**	**east**
 **south**	 **east**	**west**

Set 3

Set 2

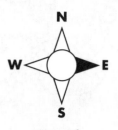

Set 1

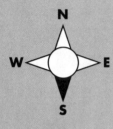

Set 3

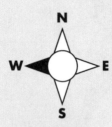

Set 2

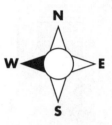

Set 1

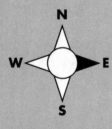

Set 3

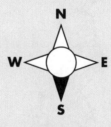

Set 2

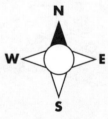

Set 1

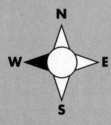

Set 3

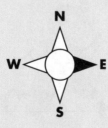

Set 2

Set 1

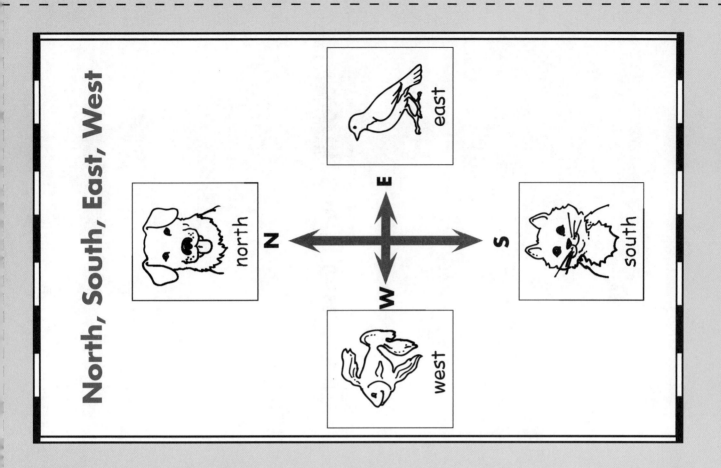

North, South, East, West

Lift the flap to check your answers.

North, South, East, West

©2005 by Evan-Moor Corp. • EMC 3716

North, South, East, West

©2005 by Evan-Moor Corp. • EMC 3716

On a Grid

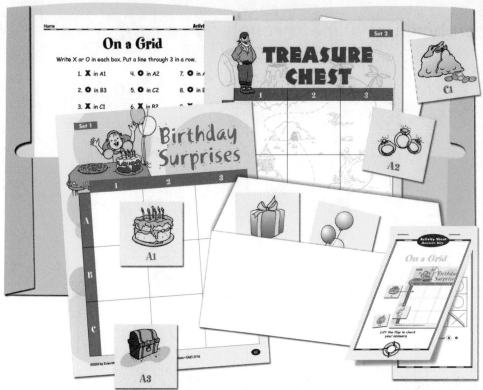

Folder Cover

Sorting Mats, Task Cards, and Activity Sheet Answer Key

Student Directions

Preparing the Center

1. Prepare a folder following the directions on page 3.

    Cover—page 63

    Student Directions—page 65

    Sorting Mats—pages 67 and 69

    Task Cards—page 71

    Activity Sheet Answer Key—page 73

2. Place the sorting mats and envelopes of cards in the right-hand pocket of the folder.

3. Reproduce a supply of the activity sheet on page 62. Place copies in the left-hand pocket of the folder.

Using the Center

1. The student takes a set of cards, the matching sorting mat, and an activity sheet.

2. The student reads each card and places it on the grid on the sorting mat.

3. The student repeats this step with the other sorting mat grid. The cards in each set are self-checking on the back.

4. Next, the student completes the grid on the activity sheet.

5. The student uses the activity sheet answer key to check his or her answers.

On a Grid

Write **X** or **O** in each box. Put a line through 3 in a row.

1. **X** in A1   4. **O** in A2   7. **O** in A3

2. **O** in B3   5. **O** in C2   8. **O** in B1

3. **X** in C1   6. **X** in B2   9. **X** in C3

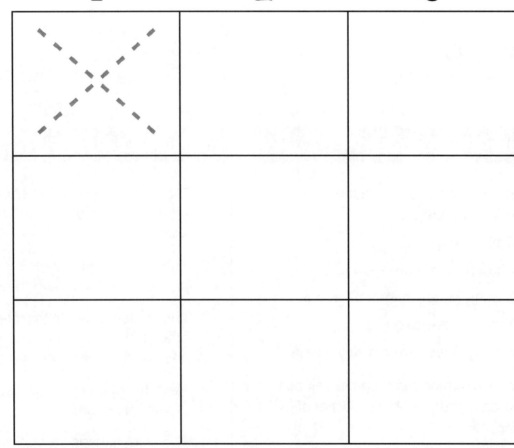

Which one made three in a row?   **X**   **O**

On a Grid

On a Grid

Follow these steps:

1. Take one set of cards and the matching mat.

2. Read a card. Put it in the correct place.

   Do the other cards the same way.

3. Turn the cards over to check your work.

4. Do the other set the same way.

5. Complete the activity sheet.

   Check your answers.

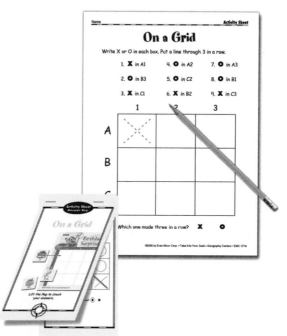

On a Grid

Set 1

©2005 by Evan-Moor Corp. • EMC 3716

TREASURE CHEST

	1	2	3
A			
B			
C	Start here		

On a Grid
Set 2

©2005 by Evan-Moor Corp. • EMC 3716

A1

B2

B3

C3

A2

C1

A2

C1

B1

B3

C2

A3

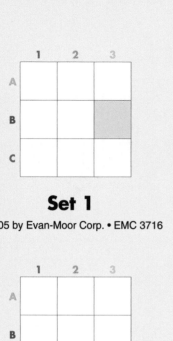

Set 1

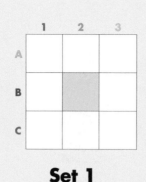

Set 1

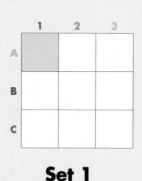

Set 1

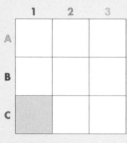

Set 1

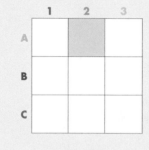

Set 1

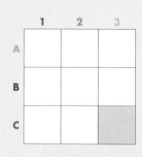

Set 1

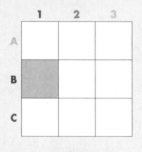

Set 2

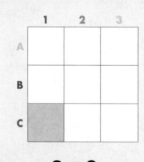

Set 2

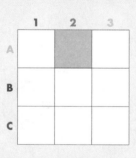

Set 2

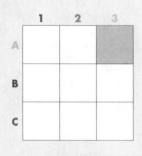

Set 2

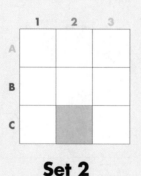

Set 2

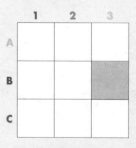

Set 2

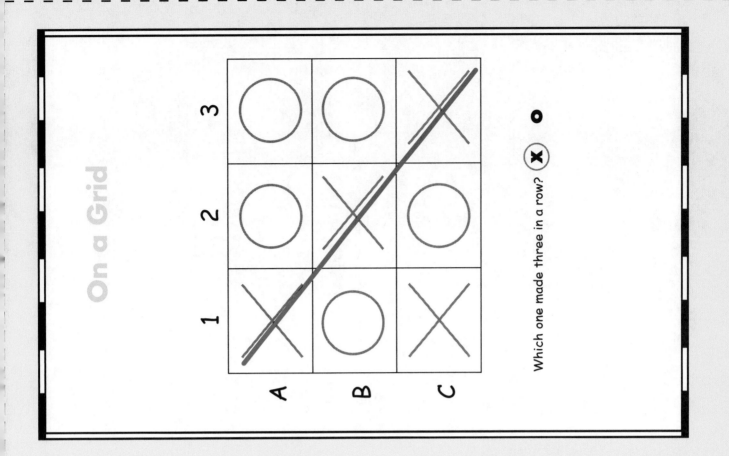

Which one made three in a row? (X) o

On a Grid

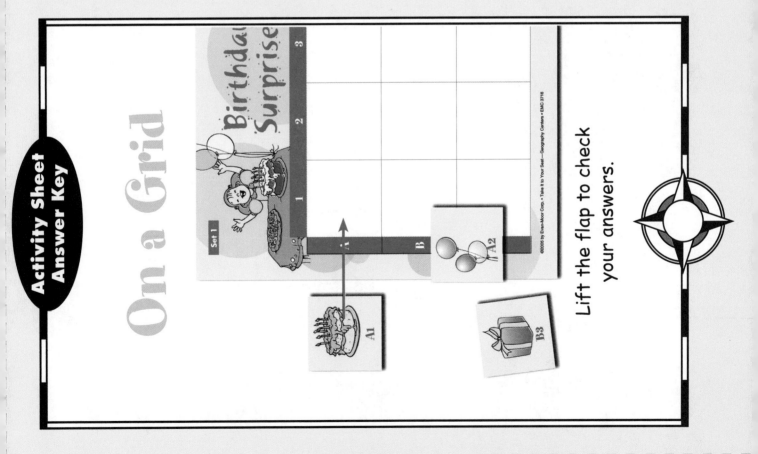

Lift the flap to check
your answers.

On a Grid

©2005 by Evan-Moor Corp. • EMC 3716

On a Grid

©2005 by Evan-Moor Corp. • EMC 3716

Parts of a Map

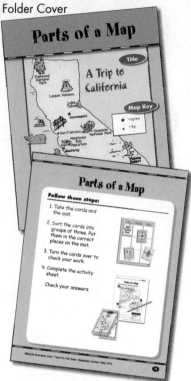

Folder Cover

Sorting Mat, Task Cards, and Activity Sheet Answer Key

Student Directions

Preparing the Center

1. Prepare a folder following the directions on page 3.

   Cover—page 77

   Student Directions—page 79

   Sorting Mat—page 81

   Task Cards—page 83

   Activity Sheet Answer Key—page 85

2. Place the sorting mat and envelope of cards in the right-hand pocket of the folder.

3. Reproduce a supply of the activity sheet on page 76. Place copies in the left-hand pocket of the folder.

Using the Center

1. The student takes the sorting mat, the envelope of cards, and an activity sheet.

2. The student removes the cards from the envelope and places them under the correct heading on the sorting mat. The cards are self-checking on the back.

3. Next, the student completes the activity sheet by labeling the parts of a map.

4. The student uses the activity sheet answer key to check his or her answers.

Parts of a Map

Name the parts. Use the word box to help you.

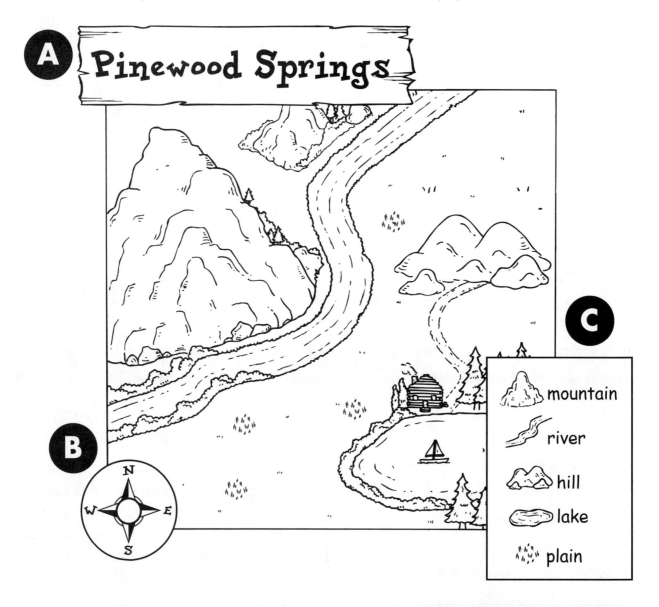

A _____

B _____

C _____

Word Box
Compass Rose
Map Key
Title

Parts of a Map

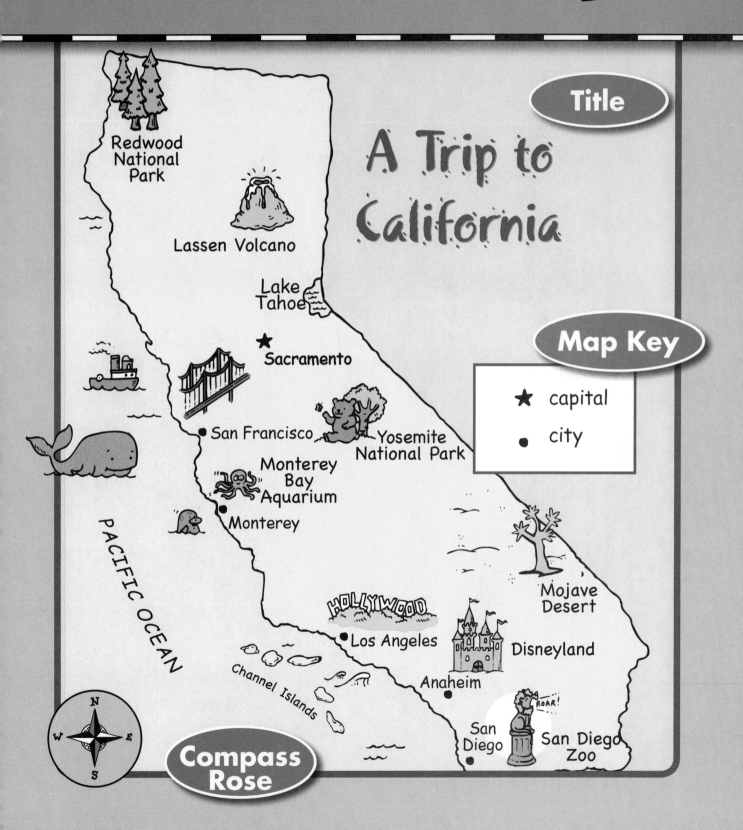

Title

A Trip to California

Map Key

★ capital
• city

Redwood National Park

Lassen Volcano

Lake Tahoe

★ Sacramento

• San Francisco

Yosemite National Park

Monterey Bay Aquarium

• Monterey

PACIFIC OCEAN

HOLLYWOOD

• Los Angeles

Channel Islands

Mojave Desert

Disneyland

• Anaheim

ROAR!

San Diego

San Diego Zoo

Compass Rose

N W E S

Parts of a Map

Follow these steps:

1. Take the cards and the mat.

2. Sort the cards into groups of three. Put them in the correct places on the mat.

3. Turn the cards over to check your work.

4. Complete the activity sheet.

   Check your answers.

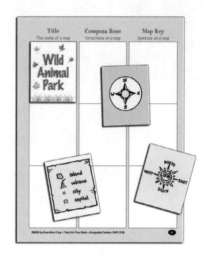

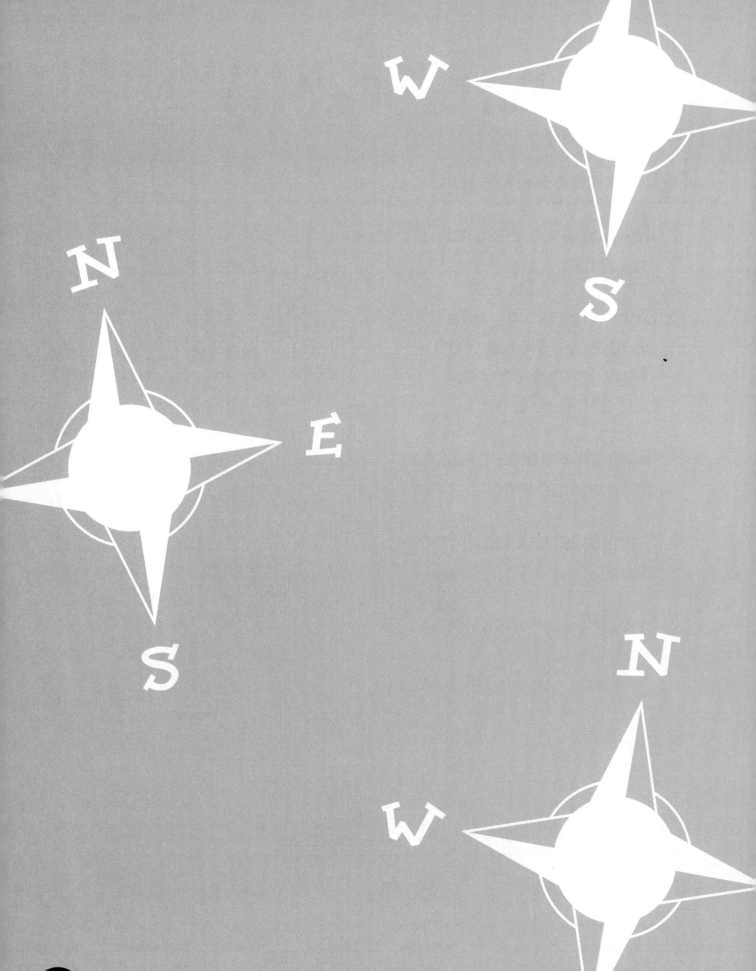

Title
The name of a map

Compass Rose
Directions on a map

Map Key
Symbols on a map

Parts of a Map

Wild Animal Park

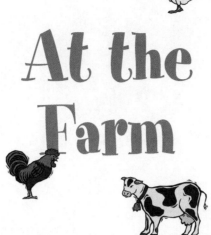

At the Farm

The World

island
volcano
city
capital

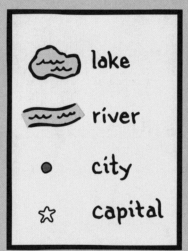

lake
river
city
capital

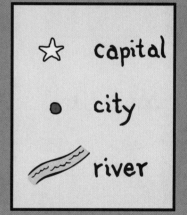

capital
city
river

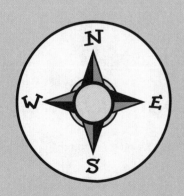

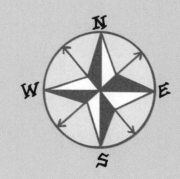

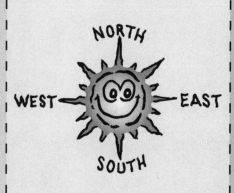

Title

Title

Title

Map Key

Map Key

Map Key

Compass Rose

Compass Rose

Compass Rose

Parts of a Map

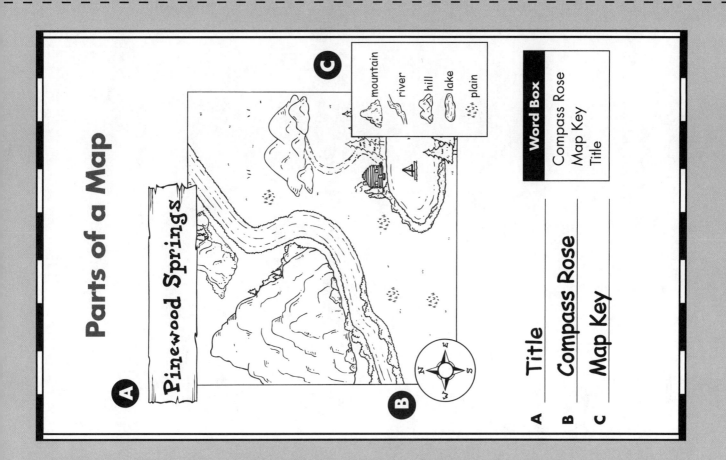

A Title

B Compass Rose

C Map Key

Word Box

Compass Rose
Map Key
Title

Activity Sheet Answer Key

Parts of a Map

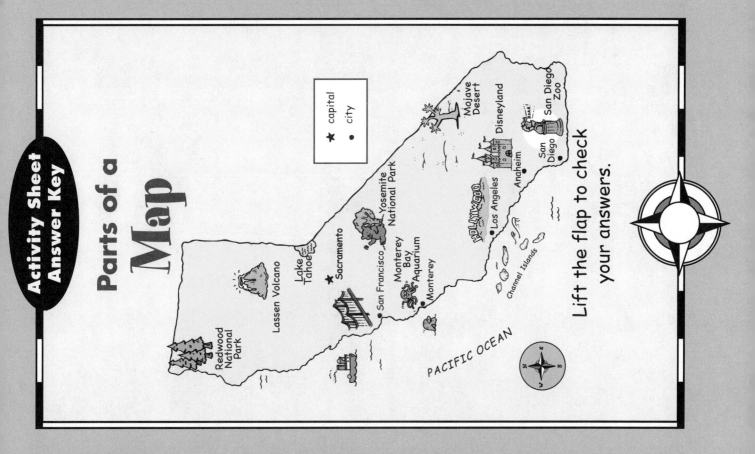

Lift the flap to check your answers.

Parts of a Map

Parts of a Map

©2005 by Evan-Moor Corp. • EMC 3716

Name It

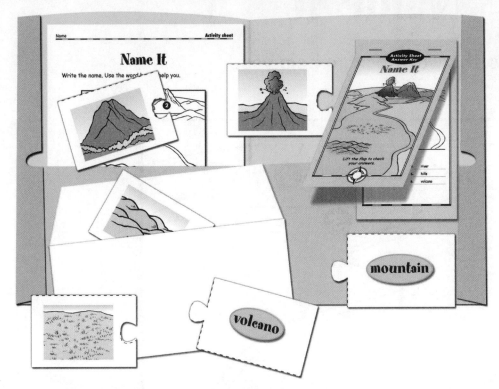

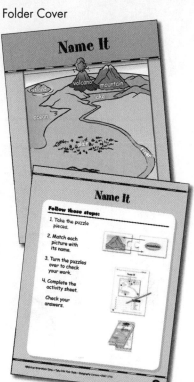

Folder Cover

Puzzle Pieces and Activity Sheet Answer Key

Student Directions

Preparing the Center

1. Prepare a folder following the directions on page 3.

   Cover—page 89

   Student Directions—page 91

   Puzzle Pieces—pages 93 and 95

   Activity Sheet Answer Key—page 97

2. Place the envelope of puzzle pieces in the right-hand pocket of the folder.

3. Reproduce a supply of the activity sheet on page 88. Place copies in the left-hand pocket of the folder.

Using the Center

1. The student takes the envelope of puzzle pieces and an activity sheet.

2. The student removes the puzzle pieces from the envelope and matches each picture with its correct name. The puzzle pieces are self-checking on the back.

3. Next, the student completes the activity sheet by writing the names of the pictures on the lines.

4. The student uses the activity sheet answer key to check his or her answers.

Name It

Write the name. Use the word box to help you.

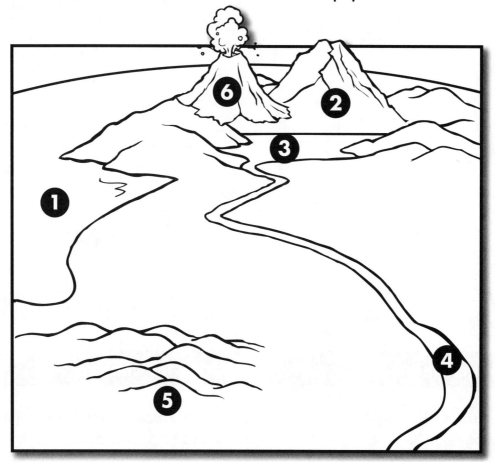

1. _____

2. _____

3. _____

4. _____

5. _____

6. _____

Word Box

hills
lake
mountain
ocean
river
volcano

Name It

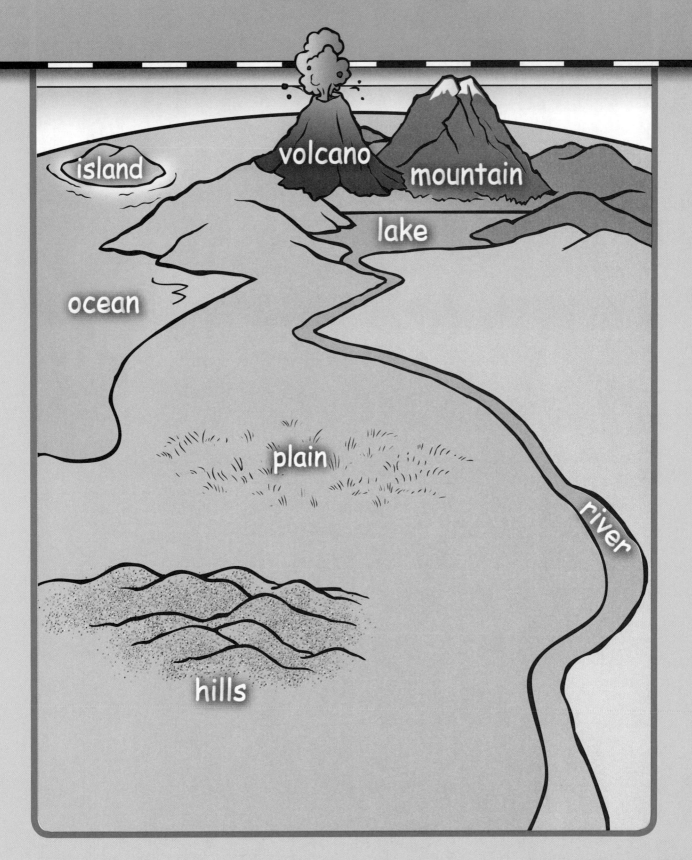

Name It

Follow these steps:

1. Take the puzzle pieces.

2. Match each picture with its name.

3. Turn the puzzles over to check your work.

4. Complete the activity sheet.

   Check your answers.

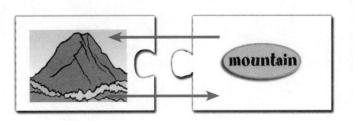

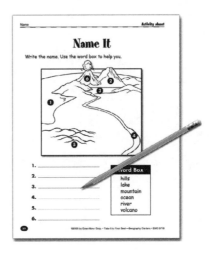

mountain

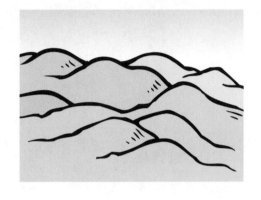

hills

volcano

plain

mountain

Name It

mountain

Name It

hills

Name It

hills

Name It

volcano

Name It

volcano

Name It

plain

Name It

plain

Name It

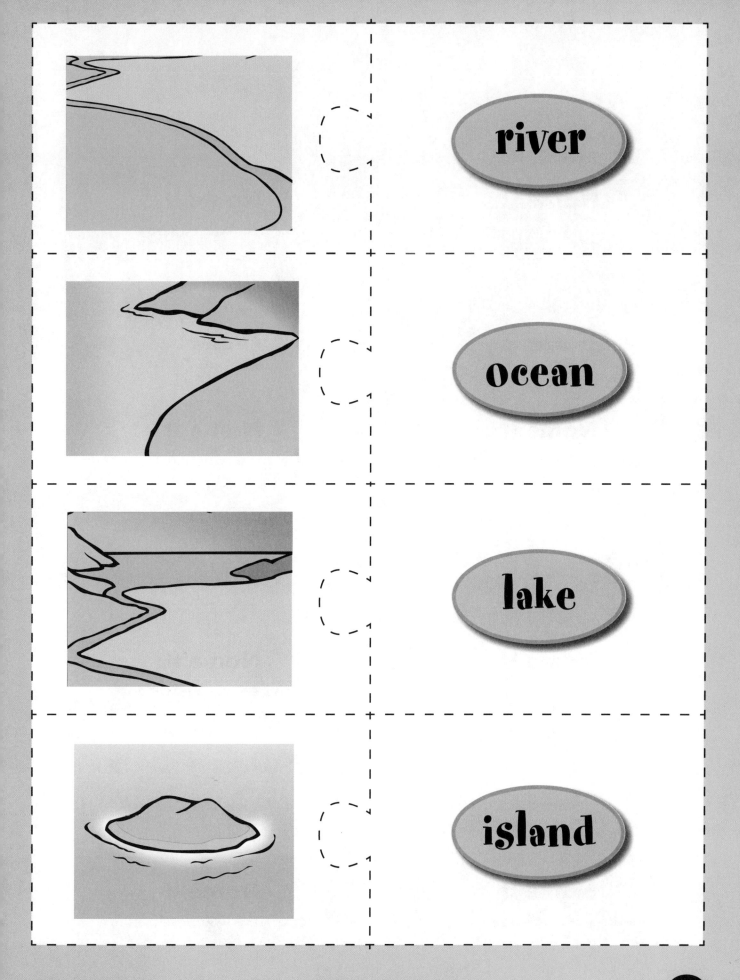

river

Name It

river

Name It

©2005 by Evan-Moor Corp. • EMC 3716

ocean

Name It

ocean

Name It

©2005 by Evan-Moor Corp. • EMC 3716

lake

Name It

lake

Name It

©2005 by Evan-Moor Corp. • EMC 3716

island

Name It

island

Name It

©2005 by Evan-Moor Corp. • EMC 3716

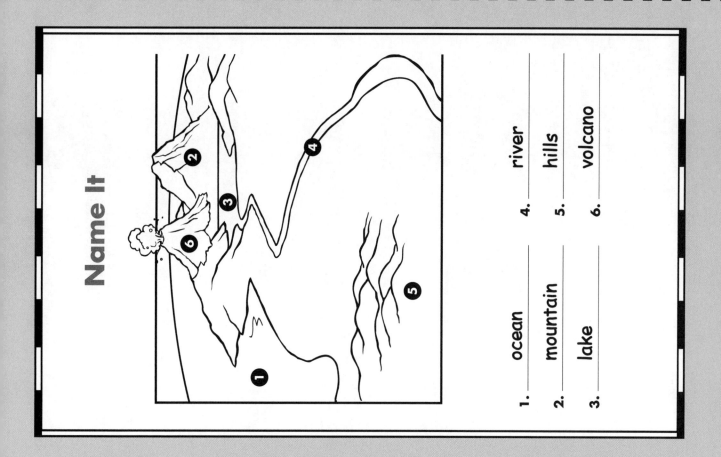

Name It

ocean 1. _____

mountain 2. _____

lake 3. _____

river 4. _____

hills 5. _____

volcano 6. _____

Name It

Lift the flap to check your answers.

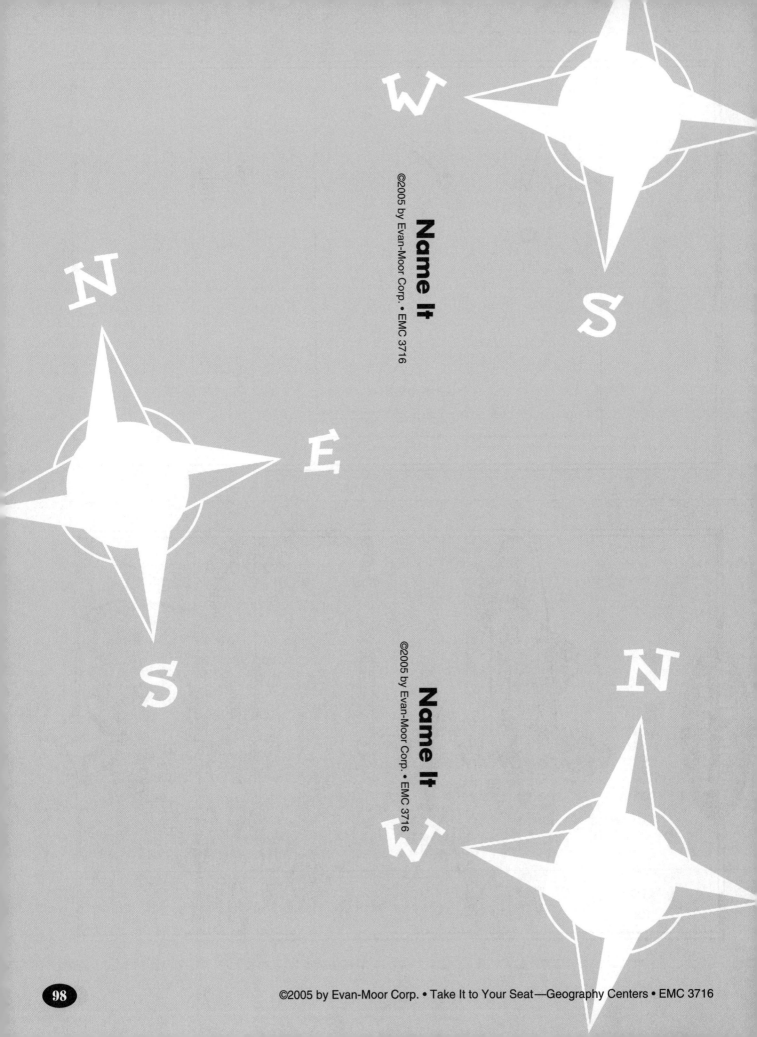

Name It

©2005 by Evan-Moor Corp. • EMC 3716

Name It

©2005 by Evan-Moor Corp. • EMC 3716

Map Keys

Folder Cover

Sorting Mats, Task Cards, and
Activity Sheet Answer Key

Student Directions

Preparing the Center

1. Prepare a folder following the
   directions on page 3.

   Cover—page 101

   Student Directions—page 103

   Sorting Mats—pages 105–111

   Task Cards—page 113

   Activity Sheet Answer Key—page 115

2. Place the sorting mats and envelopes
   of cards in the right-hand pocket of the
   folder.

3. Reproduce a supply of the activity
   sheet on page 100. Place copies in the
   left-hand pocket of the folder.

Using the Center

Note: You may divide this task in half.

1. The student takes the sorting mats,
   the envelopes of task cards, and
   an activity sheet.

2. Then the student lays out all the
   sorting mats faceup and matches a key
   to each of the maps. The number on
   the back of the key matches the map
   number.

3. Next, the student completes the activity
   sheet by drawing a line from each map
   to its key.

4. The student uses the activity sheet
   answer key to check his or her answers.

Map Keys

Draw a line to make a match.

Map Key	
 volcano	
island	
waterfall	

Map Key	
★	capital
◉	city
– – –	state border

Map Key			
Animals Raised		**Plants Grown**	
Beef Cattle		Corn	
Dairy Cows		Soybeans	
Hogs			

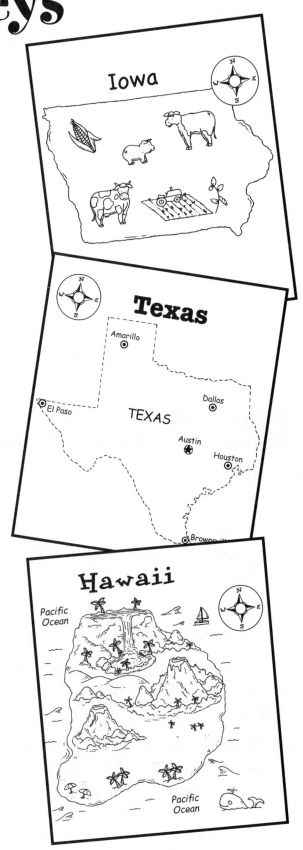

Iowa

Texas

Amarillo
El Paso   Dallas
TEXAS
Austin
Houston
Brownsville

Hawaii

Pacific Ocean

Pacific Ocean

Map Keys

 plains

 mountain range

 mountain peak

 river

 city

 capital

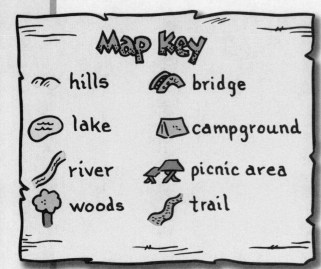

Map Key

hills   bridge

lake   campground

river   picnic area

woods   trail

Map Key

bay

gulf

lake

river

• city

★ capital

MAP KEY

 sunny

 partly cloudy

 snow

 thunderstorms

 rain

 50° temperature

Map Key

 ★ capital

 • city

 state border

 river

Map Keys

Follow these steps:

1. Take the cards and maps.

2. Match each key with its map.

3. Turn the cards over to check your work.

4. Complete the activity sheet.

   Check your answers.

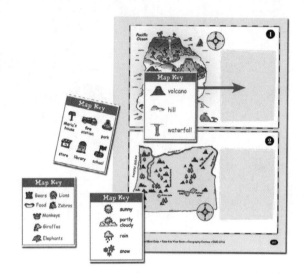

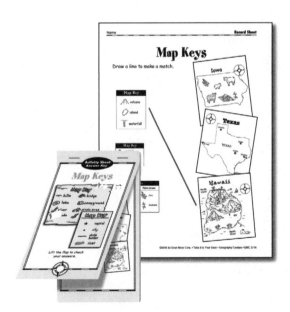

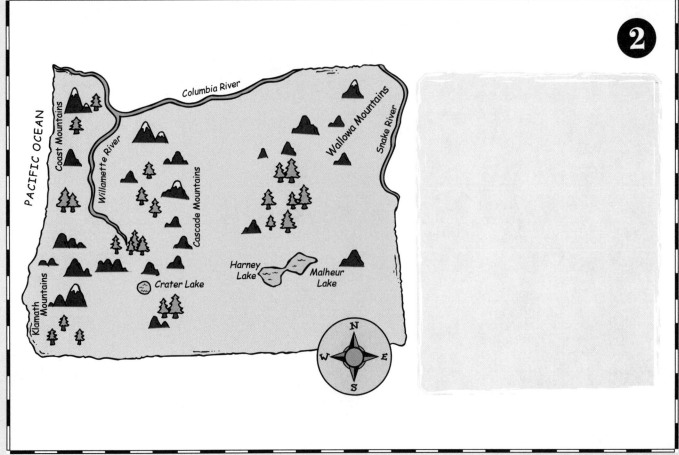

Map Keys

©2005 by Evan-Moor Corp. • EMC 3716

Map Keys

©2005 by Evan-Moor Corp. • EMC 3716

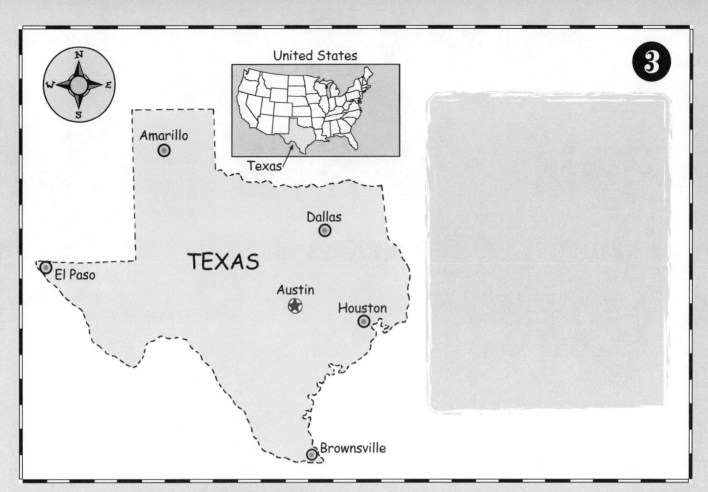

United States

Texas

Amarillo

Dallas

TEXAS

El Paso

Austin

Houston

Brownsville

Maria's Neighborhood

High Street

Main Street

Safe Street

Book Street

Low Street

Map Keys

©2005 by Evan-Moor Corp. • EMC 3716

Map Keys

©2005 by Evan-Moor Corp. • EMC 3716

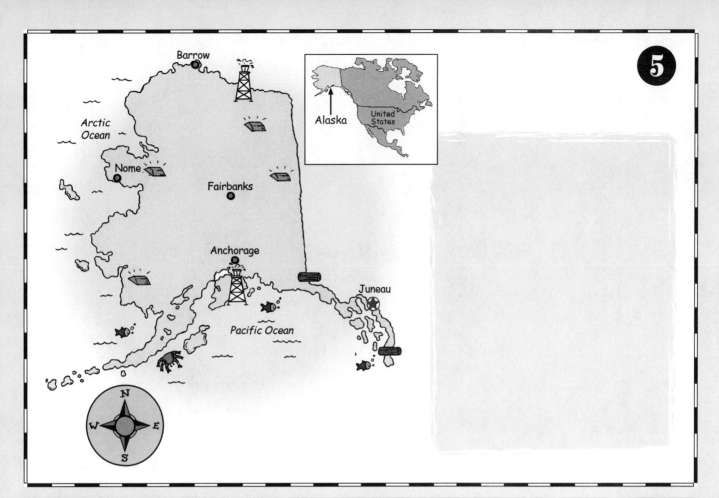

5

Central City Zoo

Map Keys

©2005 by Evan-Moor Corp. • EMC 3716

Map Keys

©2005 by Evan-Moor Corp. • EMC 3716

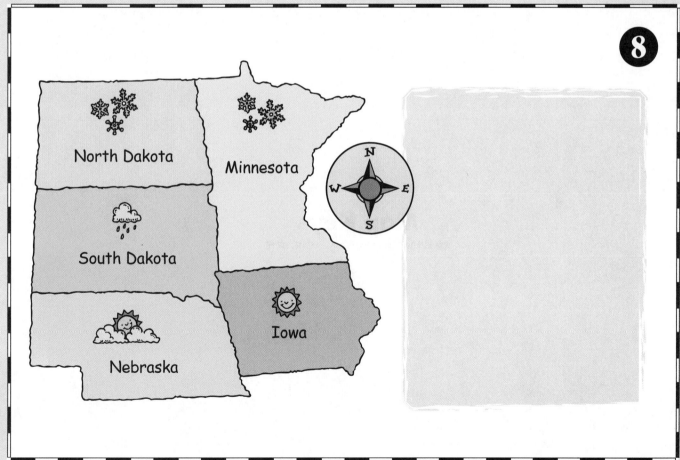

Map Keys

Map Keys

Map Key

 volcano

 hills

 waterfall

Map Key

 forest

 lake

 mountain

 river

Map Key

 capital

 city

_ _ _ state border

Map Key

 Maria's house
 fire station
 park

 store
 library
 school

Map Key

 Fish
 Oil

 Crab
 Gold

 Capital
 City

 Lumber

Map Key

 Bears
 Lions

Food
Zebras

Monkeys

Giraffes

Elephants

Map Key

Animals Raised

Beef Cattle   Hogs   Dairy Cows

Plants Grown

 Corn    Soybeans

Map Key

 sunny

 partly cloudy

 rain

 snow

113

3

Map Keys

2

Map Keys

1

Map Keys

6

Map Keys

5

Map Keys

4

Map Keys

8

Map Keys

7

Map Keys

Map Keys

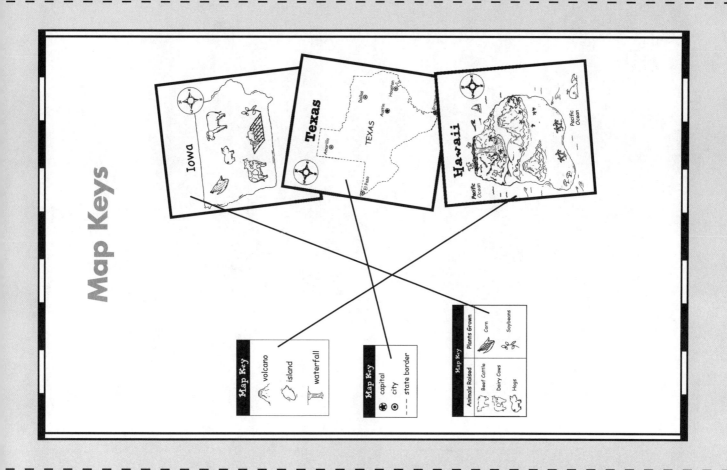

Map Key
- volcano
- island
- waterfall

Map Key
- capital
- city
- state border

Map Key

Animals Raised			Plants Grown	
Beef Cattle	Dairy Cows	Hogs	Corn	Soybeans

Map Keys

Map Key
- hills
- lake
- river
- woods
- bridge
- campground
- picnic area

Map Key
- ★ capital
- • city
- state border
- river

Lift the flap to check your answers.

Map Keys

Map Keys

Our World

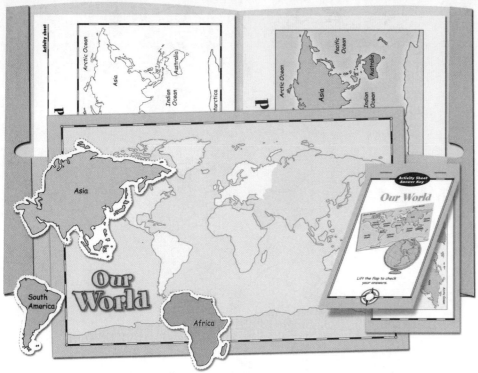

Folder Cover

Sorting Mat, Puzzle Pieces, and Activity Sheet Answer Key

Student Directions

Preparing the Center

1. Prepare a folder following the directions on page 3.

   Cover—page 119

   Student Directions—page 121

   Sorting Mat—pages 123 and 125

   Puzzle Pieces—pages 127 and 129

   Activity Sheet Answer Key—page 133

2. Laminate the world map on page 131. Place it in the right-hand pocket of the folder for student reference, along with the sorting mat and envelope of puzzle pieces.

3. Reproduce a supply of the activity sheet on page 118. Place copies in the left-hand pocket of the folder.

Using the Center

1. The student takes the sorting mat, the envelope of puzzle pieces, and an activity sheet.

2. Then the student places the puzzle pieces correctly on the world map. The student uses the laminated world map on page 131 to check his or her work.

3. Next, the student completes the activity sheet by coloring each continent the same color as it is on the sorting mat.

4. The student uses the activity sheet answer key to check his or her answers.

Our World

Color the continents to match the sorting mat.

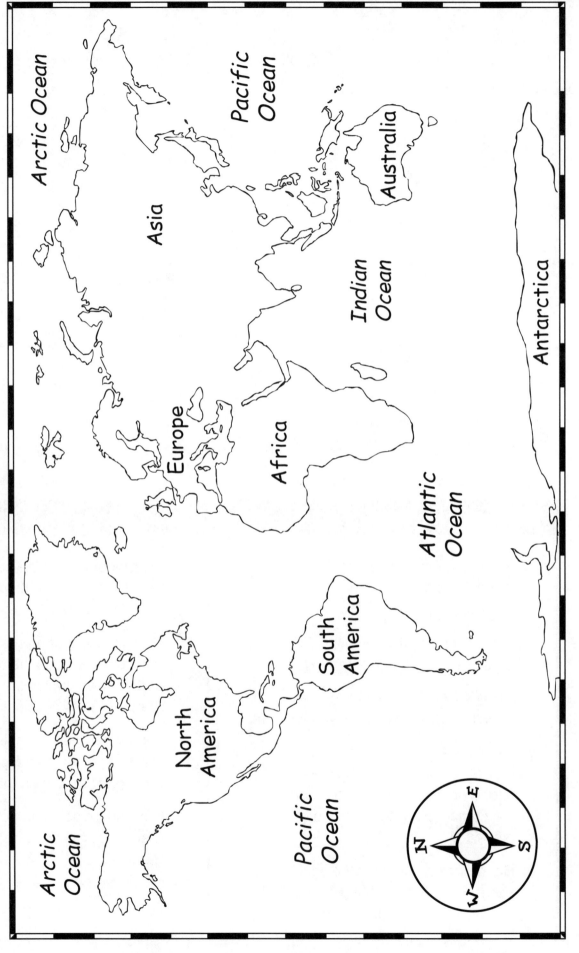

Arctic Ocean

Pacific Ocean

Australia

Asia

Indian Ocean

Antarctica

Europe

Africa

Atlantic Ocean

South America

North America

Arctic Ocean

Pacific Ocean

Our World

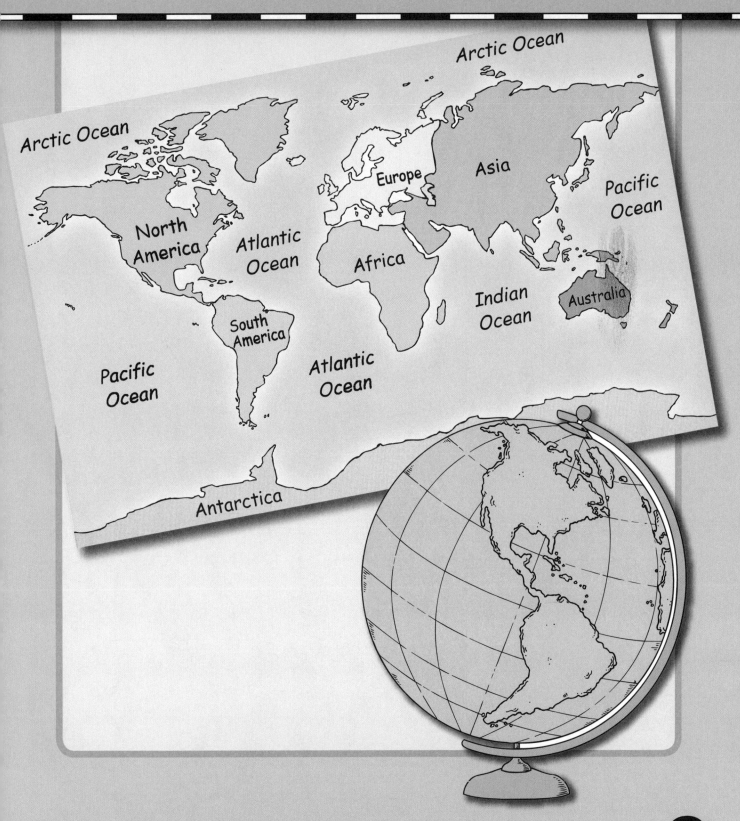

Our World

Follow these steps:

1. Take the puzzle pieces and the mat.

2. Put the continents in the correct places on the mat.

3. Look at the labeled world map to check your work.

4. Complete the activity sheet.

   Check your answers.

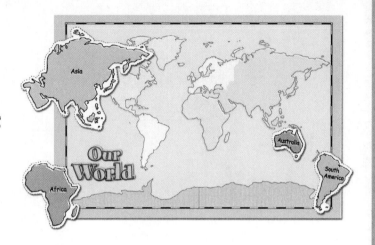

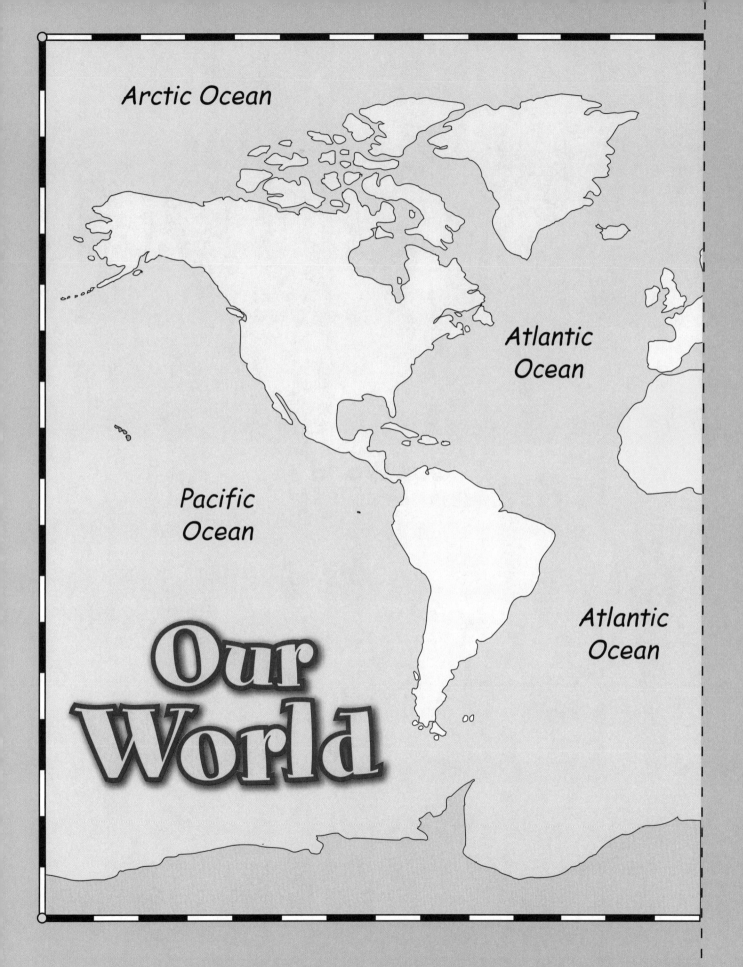

Arctic Ocean

Atlantic
Ocean

Pacific
Ocean

Atlantic
Ocean

Our
World

Our World

©2005 by Evan-Moor Corp. • EMC 3716

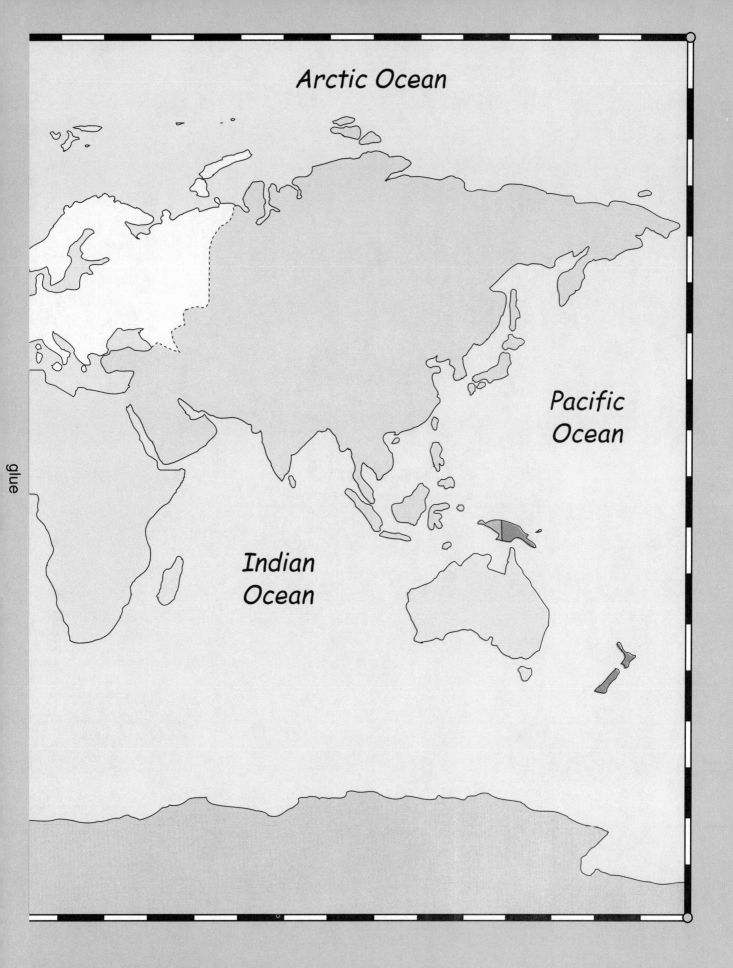

Arctic Ocean

Pacific
Ocean

Indian
Ocean

glue

Our World

©2005 by Evan-Moor Corp. • EMC 3716

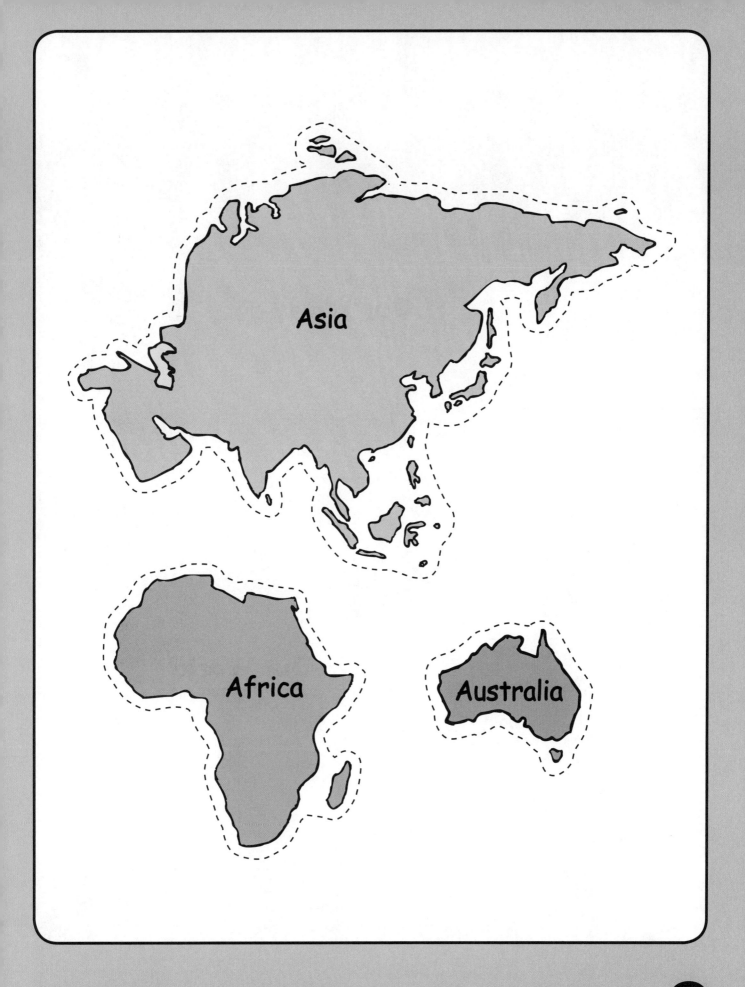

Our World

©2005 by Evan-Moor Corp.
EMC 3716

Our World

©2005 by Evan-Moor Corp.
EMC 3716

Our World

©2005 by Evan-Moor Corp.
EMC 3716

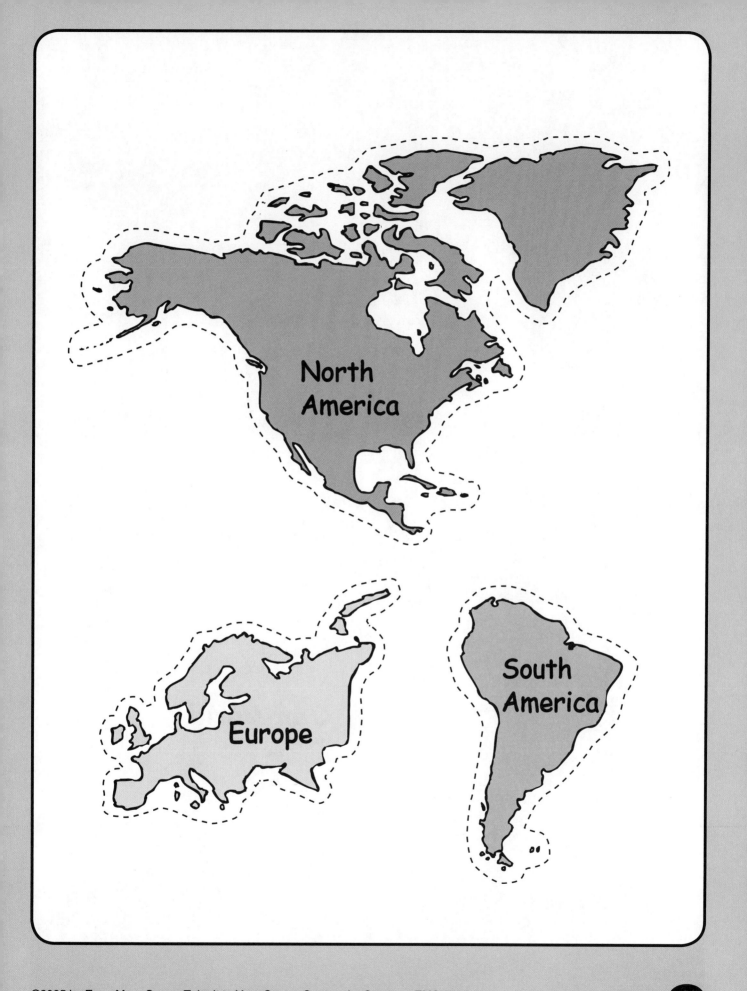

North America

Europe

South America

Our World

©2005 by Evan-Moor Corp.
EMC 3716

Our World

©2005 by Evan-Moor Corp.
EMC 3716

Our World

©2005 by Evan-Moor Corp.
EMC 3716

Our World

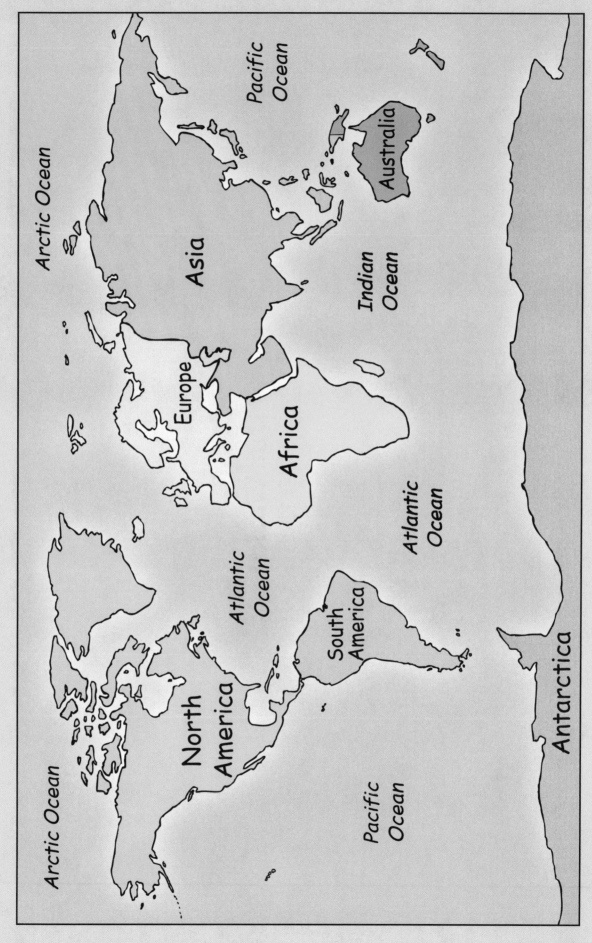

Pacific Ocean

Arctic Ocean

Asia

Australia

Indian Ocean

Europe

Africa

Atlantic Ocean

Atlantic Ocean

South America

North America

Arctic Ocean

Pacific Ocean

Antarctica

Our World

©2005 by Evan-Moor Corp.
EMC 3716

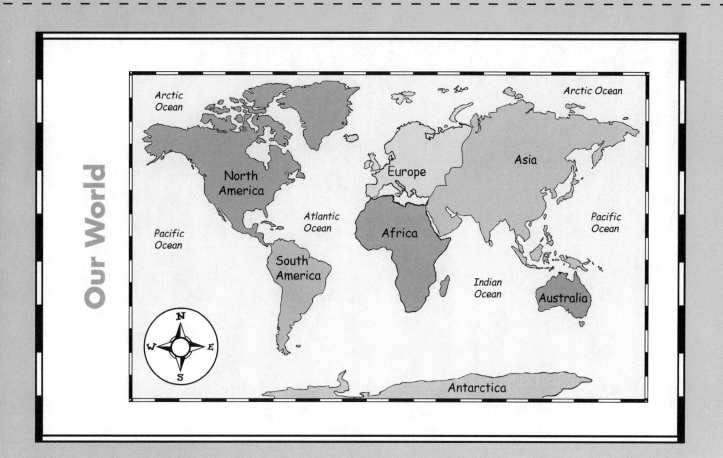

Our World

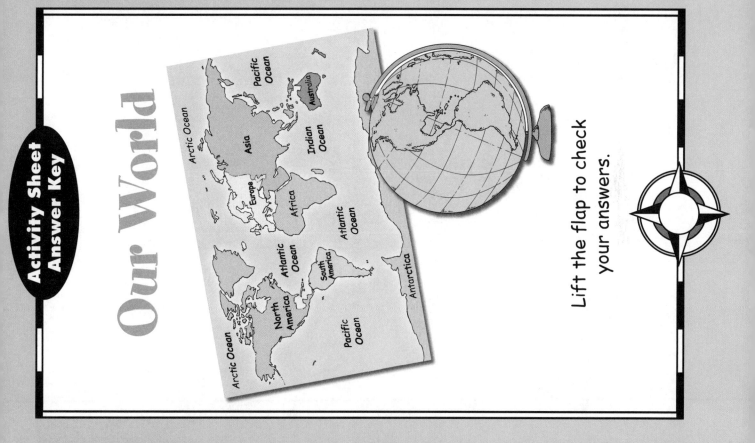

Lift the flap to check your answers.

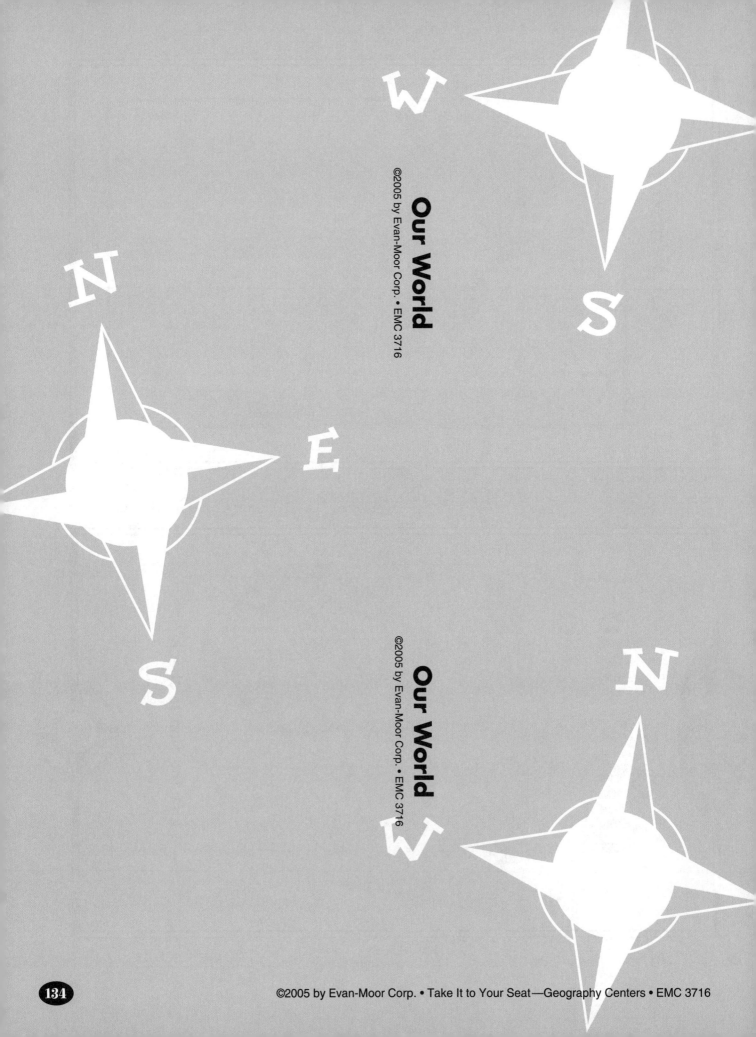

W

S

©2005 by Evan-Moor Corp. • EMC 3716

Our World

N

E

S

©2005 by Evan-Moor Corp. • EMC 3716

Our World

N

W

North America

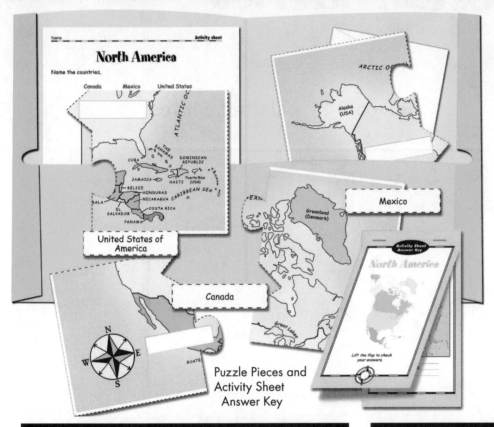

Puzzle Pieces and
Activity Sheet
Answer Key

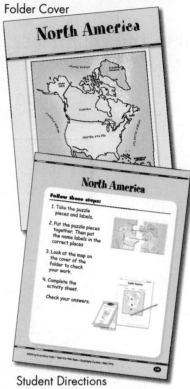

Folder Cover

Student Directions

Preparing the Center

1. Prepare a folder following the directions on page 3.

    Cover—page 137

    Student Directions—page 139

    Puzzle Pieces—pages 141 and 143

    Activity Sheet Answer Key—page 145

2. Place the envelope of puzzle pieces in the right-hand pocket of the folder.

3. Reproduce a supply of the activity sheet on page 136. Place copies in the left-hand pocket of the folder.

Using the Center

1. The student takes the envelope of puzzle pieces and an activity sheet.

2. Then the student correctly puts the puzzle pieces together to make North America and places name labels in the correct locations on the map. The student uses the folder cover to check his or her work.

3. Next, the student completes the activity sheet by writing the names of Canada, the United States, and Mexico on the lines.

4. The student uses the activity sheet answer key to check his or her answers.

North America

Name the countries.

Canada   Mexico   United States

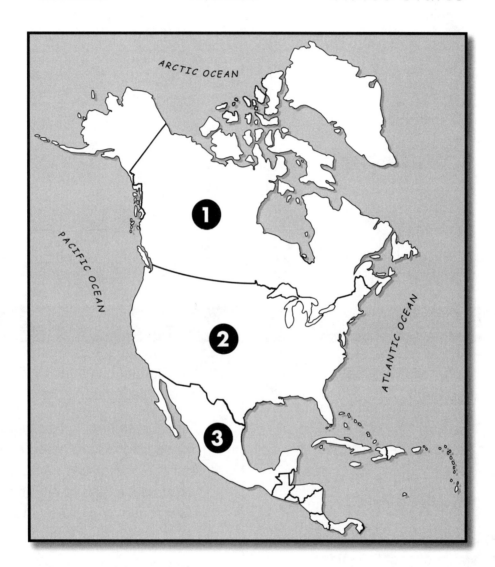

1. _____

2. _____

3. _____

North America

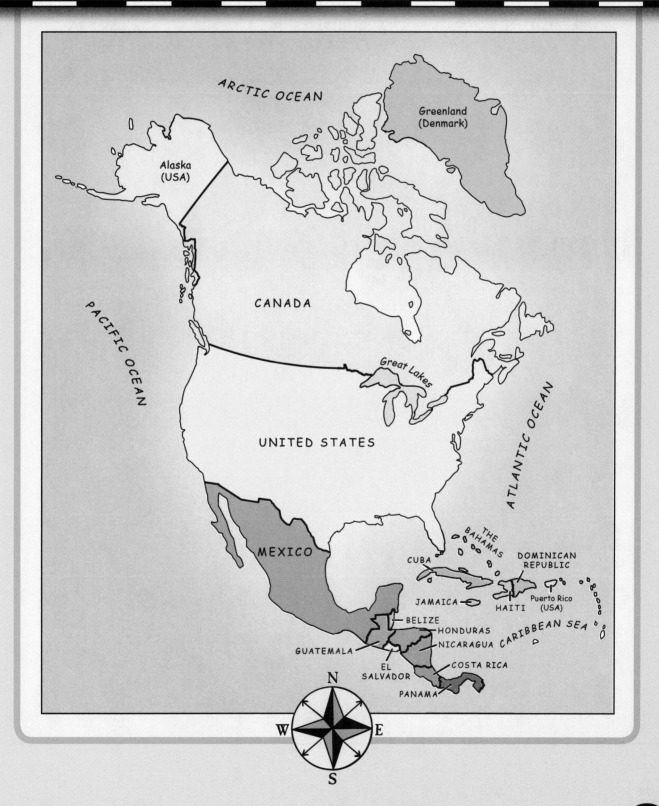

ARCTIC OCEAN

Greenland (Denmark)

Alaska (USA)

PACIFIC OCEAN

CANADA

Great Lakes

UNITED STATES

ATLANTIC OCEAN

MEXICO

THE BAHAMAS

CUBA

DOMINICAN REPUBLIC

JAMAICA

HAITI

Puerto Rico (USA)

BELIZE

HONDURAS

NICARAGUA

CARIBBEAN SEA

GUATEMALA

COSTA RICA

EL SALVADOR

PANAMA

N
W E
S

North America

Follow these steps:

1. Take the puzzle pieces and labels.

2. Put the puzzle pieces together. Then put the name labels in the correct places.

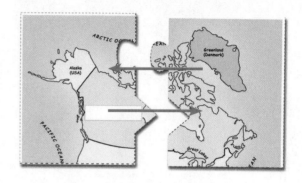

3. Look at the map on the cover of the folder to check your work.

4. Complete the activity sheet.

   Check your answers.

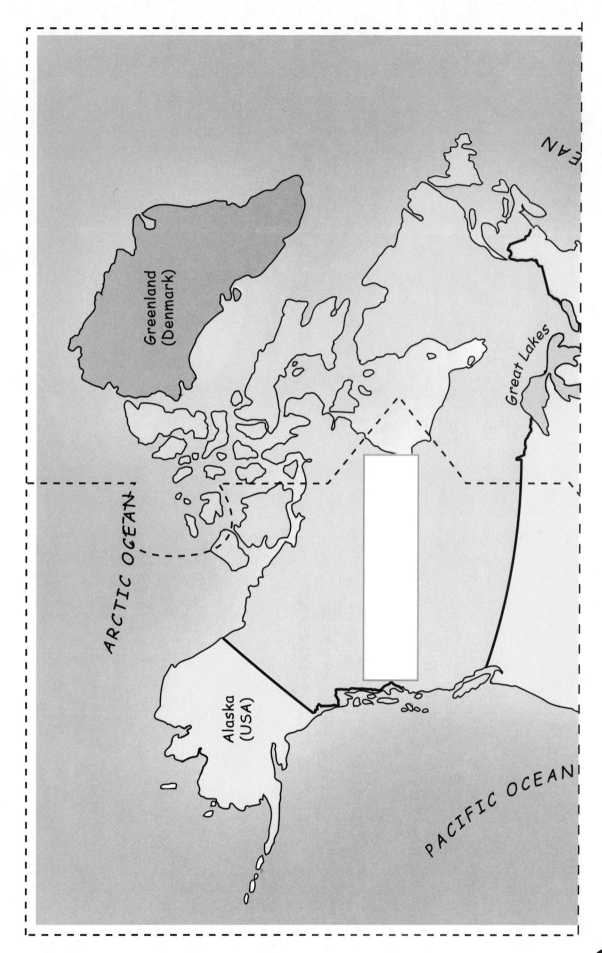

North America

©2005 by Evan-Moor Corp. • EMC 3716

North America

©2005 by Evan-Moor Corp. • EMC 3716

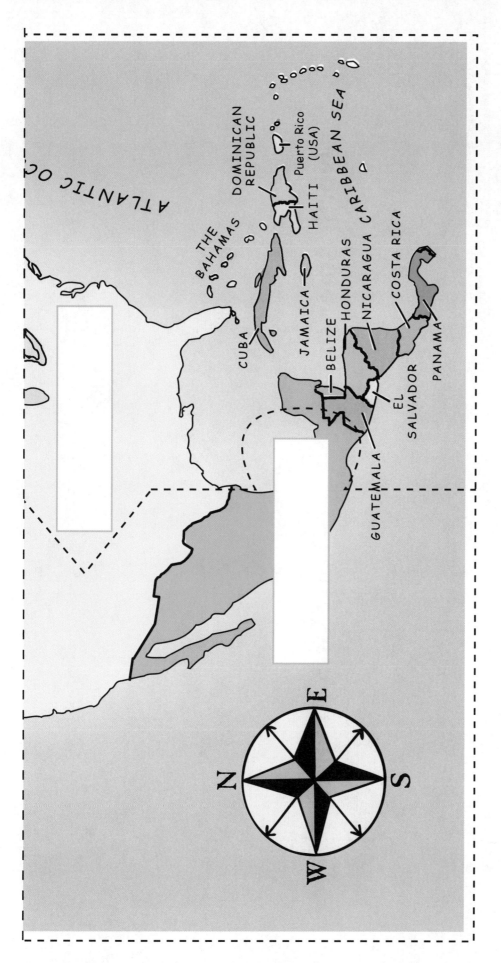

THE BAHAMAS

CUBA

JAMAICA

DOMINICAN REPUBLIC

Puerto Rico (USA)

HAITI

CARIBBEAN SEA

ATLANTIC OC

BELIZE

HONDURAS

NICARAGUA

COSTA RICA

EL SALVADOR

PANAMA

GUATEMALA

N E S W

Canada

United States of America

Mexico

North America

2005 by Evan-Moor Corp. • EMC 3716

2005 by Evan-Moor Corp. • EMC 3716

North America

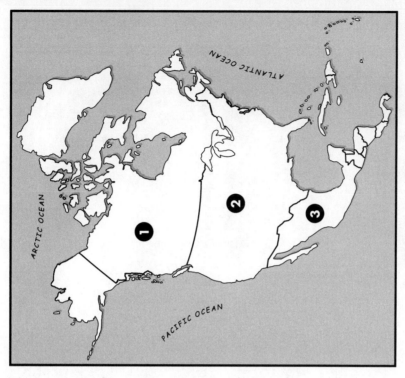

1. Canada
2. United States
3. Mexico

North America

Lift the flap to check your answers.

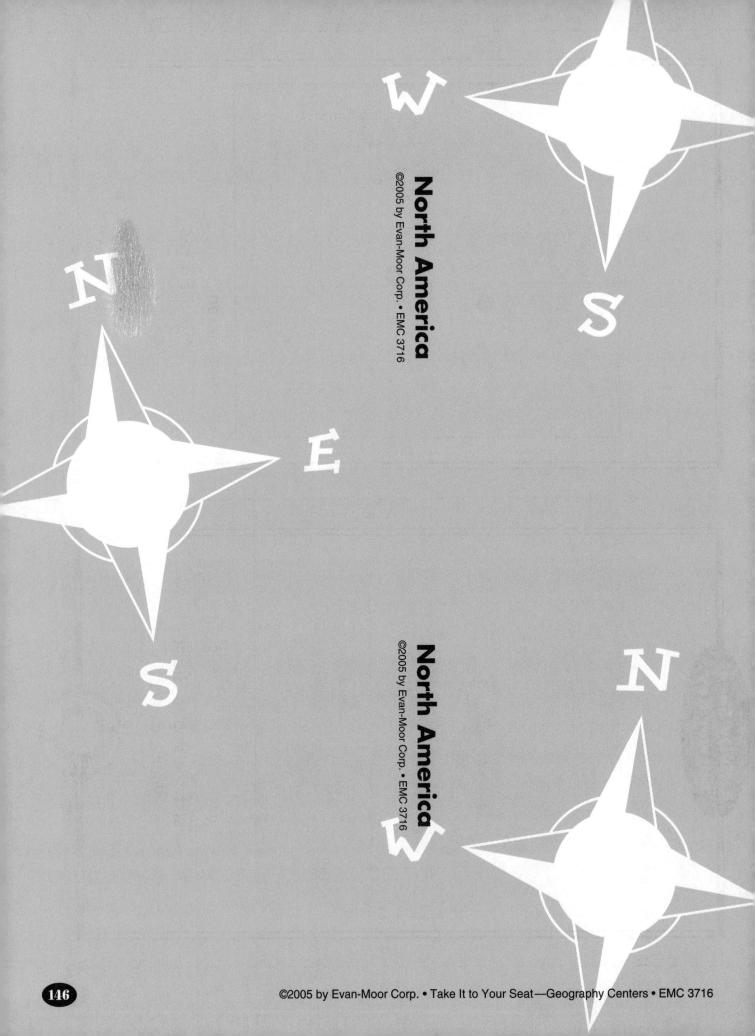

North America

©2005 by Evan-Moor Corp. • EMC 3716

North America

©2005 by Evan-Moor Corp. • EMC 3716

United States of America

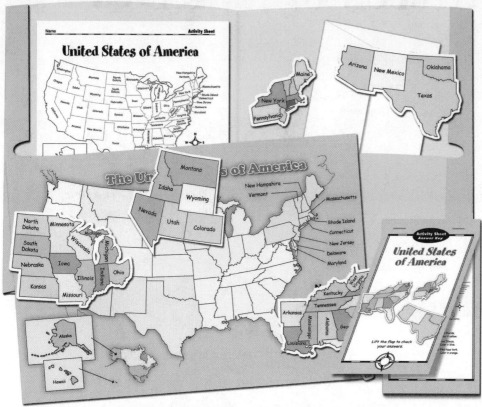

Folder Cover

Student Directions

Sorting Mat, Puzzle Pieces, and Activity Sheet Answer Key

Preparing the Center

1. Prepare a folder following the directions on page 3.

    Cover—page 149

    Student Directions—page 151

    Sorting Mat—pages 153 and 155

    Puzzle Pieces—pages 157–161

    Activity Sheet Answer Key—page 163

2. Place the sorting mat and envelope of puzzle pieces in the right-hand pocket of the folder.

3. Reproduce a supply of the activity sheet on page 148. Place copies in the left-hand pocket of the folder.

Using the Center

1. The student takes the sorting mat, the envelope of puzzle pieces, and an activity sheet.

2. Then the student puts the puzzle pieces on the map to make the United States.

3. Next, the student completes the activity sheet by coloring in some of the states as directed.

4. The student uses the activity sheet answer key to check his or her answers.

United States of America

The United States is a large country.
It has 50 states.

1. Find California.
   Color it pink.

2. Find Texas.
   Color it green.

3. Find Montana.
   Color it purple.

4. Find Florida.
   Color it yellow.

5. Find Illinois.
   Color it blue.

6. Find New York.
   Color it orange.

United States of America

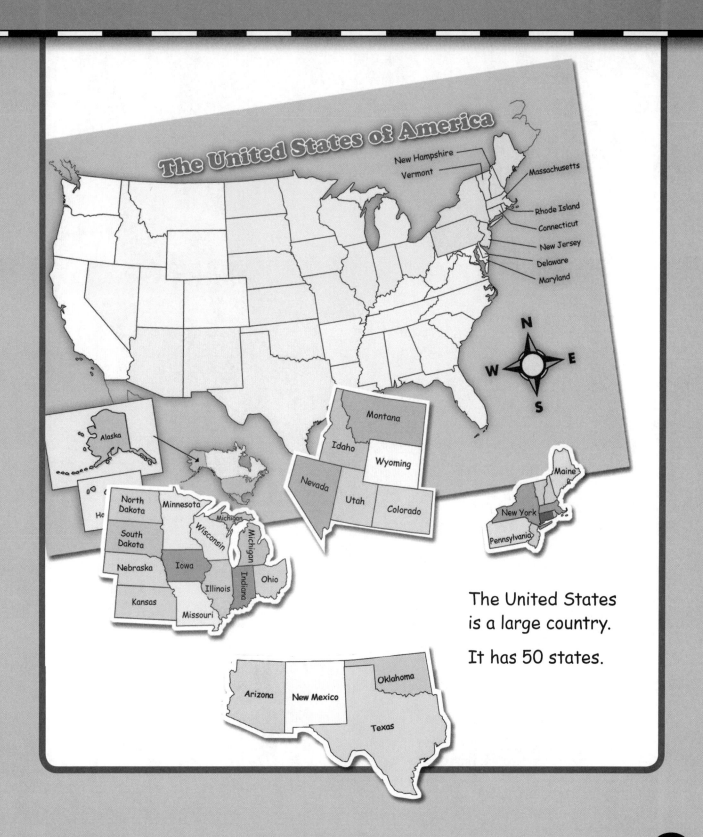

The United States is a large country.

It has 50 states.

United States of America

Follow these steps:

1. Take the puzzle pieces and the mat.

2. Put the puzzle pieces in the correct places on the mat.

3. Complete the activity sheet.

   Check your answers.

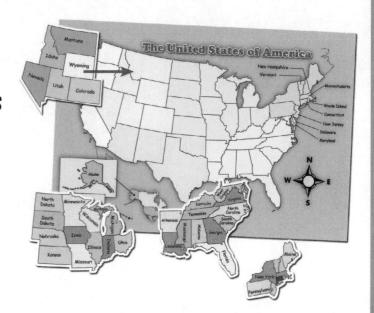

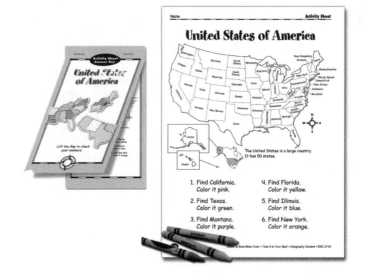

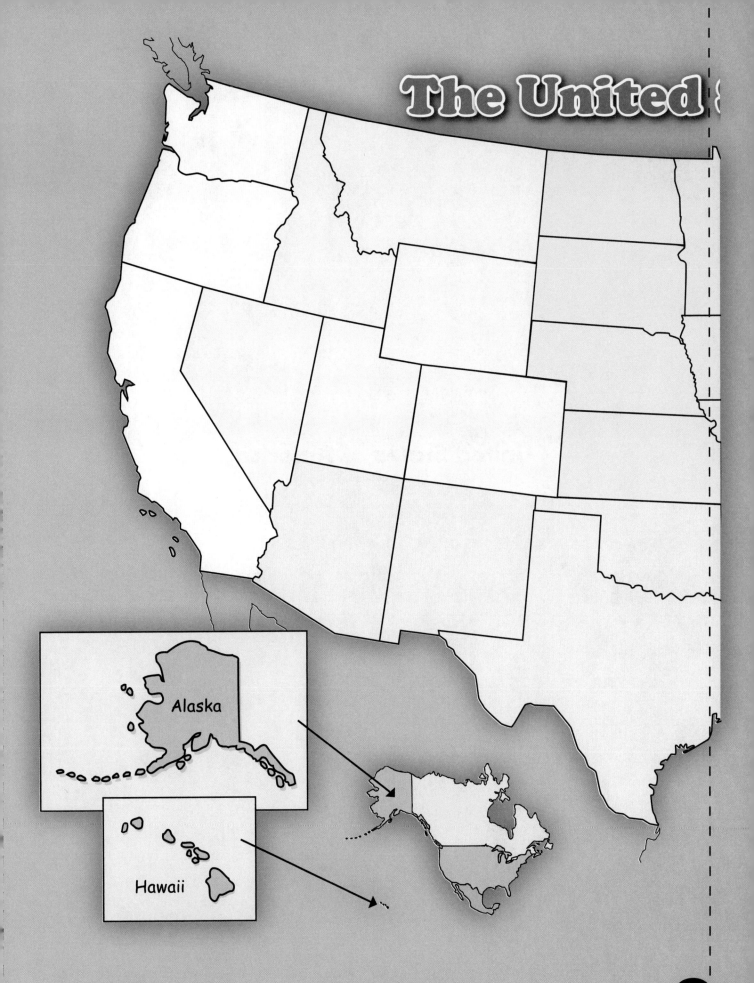

Alaska

Hawaii

United States of America

©2005 by Evan-Moor Corp. • EMC 3716

States of America

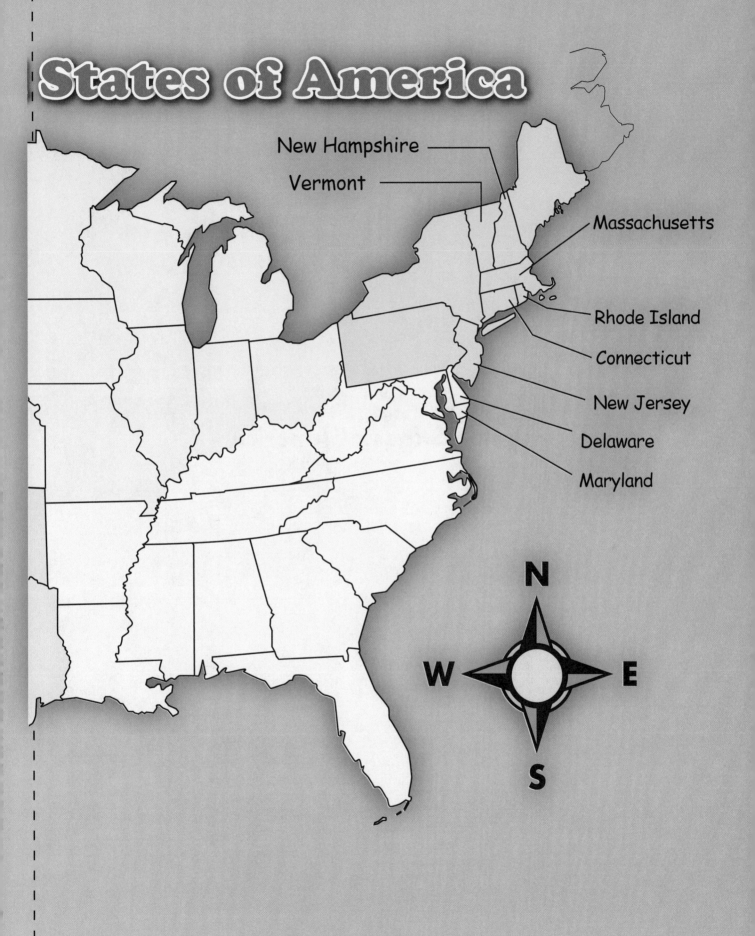

New Hampshire

Vermont

Massachusetts

Rhode Island

Connecticut

New Jersey

Delaware

Maryland

N

W   E

S

United States of America

©2005 by Evan-Moor Corp. • EMC 3716

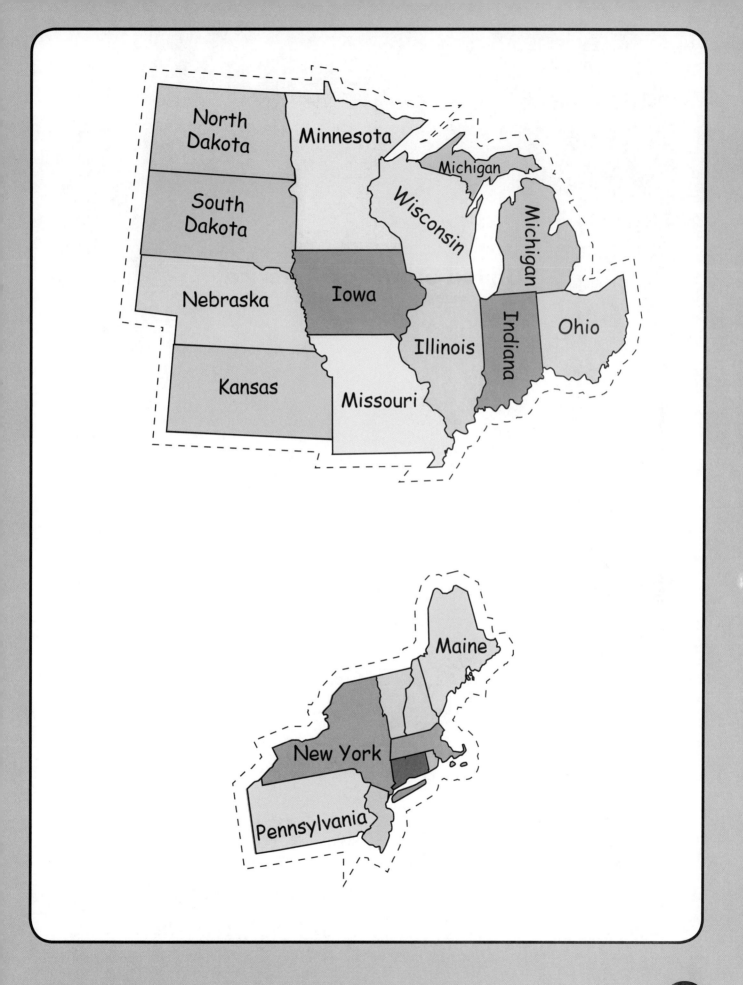

United States of America

United States of America

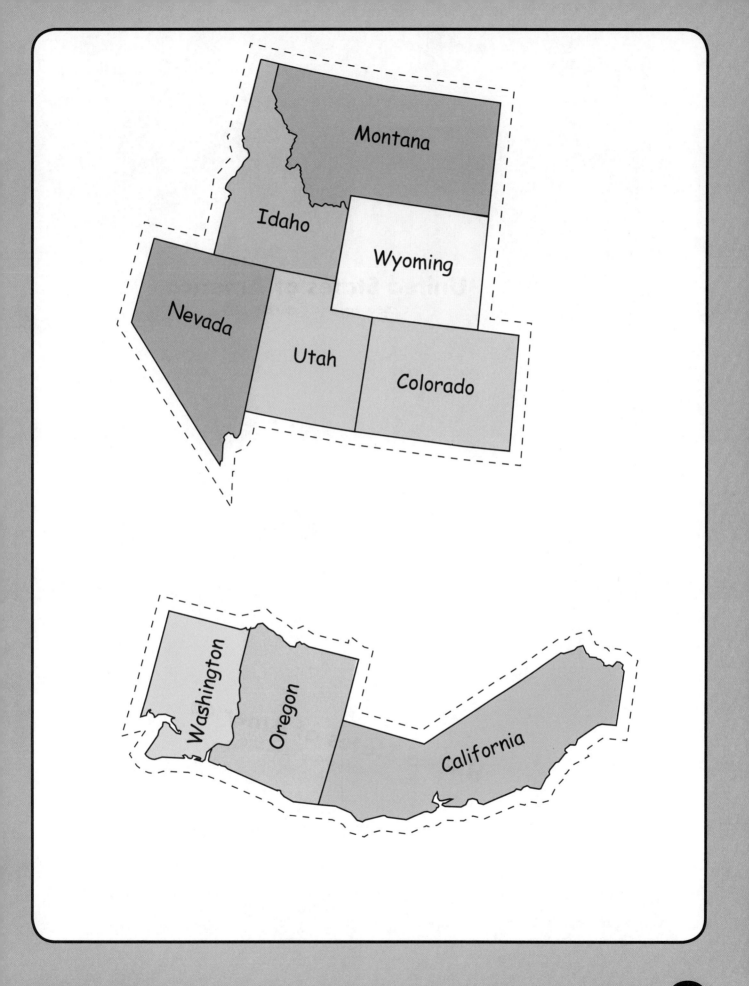

United States of America

©2005 by Evan-Moor Corp. • EMC 3716

United States of America

©2005 by Evan-Moor Corp. • EMC 3716

United States of America

©2005 by Evan-Moor Corp. • EMC 3716

United States of America

©2005 by Evan-Moor Corp. • EMC 3716

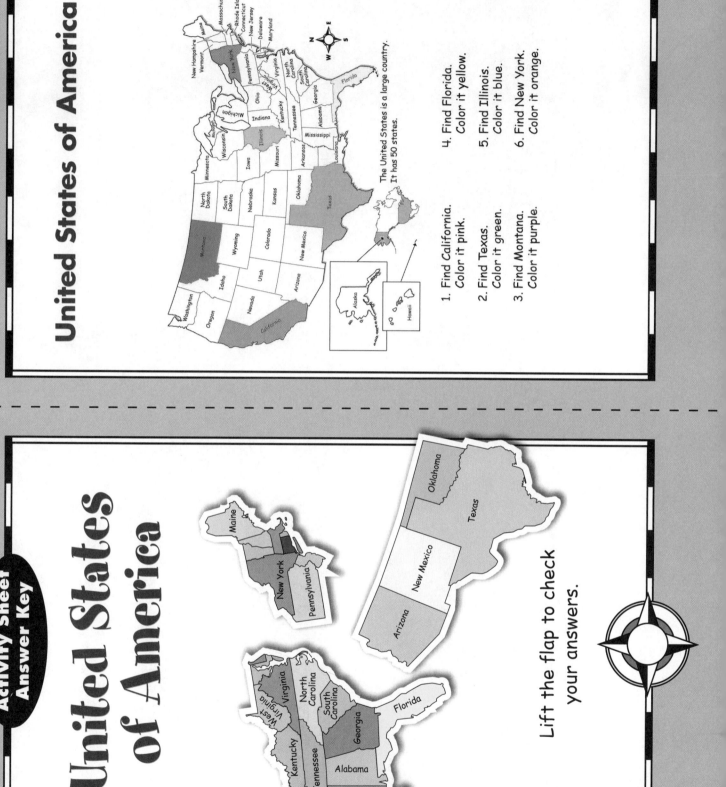

United States of America

The United States is a large country. It has 50 states.

1. Find California.
   Color it pink.

2. Find Texas.
   Color it green.

3. Find Montana.
   Color it purple.

4. Find Florida.
   Color it yellow.

5. Find Illinois.
   Color it blue.

6. Find New York.
   Color it orange.

United States of America

Lift the flap to check your answers.

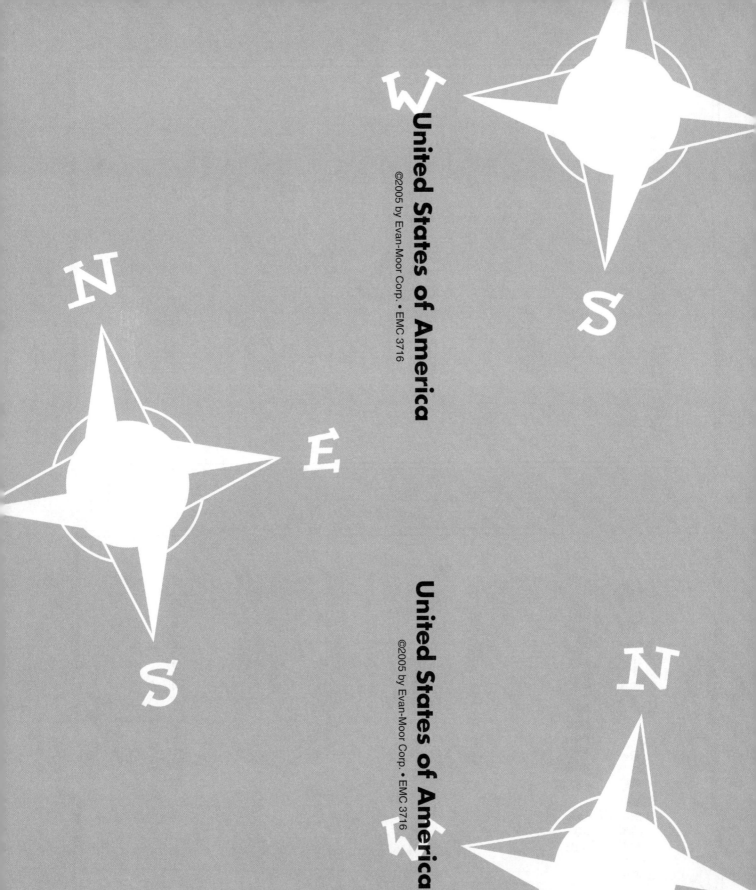

United States of America

©2005 by Evan-Moor Corp. • EMC 3716

United States of America

©2005 by Evan-Moor Corp. • EMC 3716

Make a Map

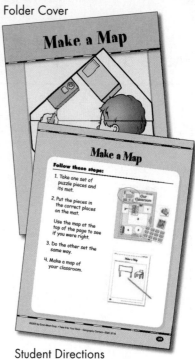

Folder Cover

Sorting Mats and
Puzzle Pieces

Student Directions

Preparing the Center

1. Prepare a folder following the directions on page 3.

    Cover—page 167

    Student Directions—page 169

    Sorting Mats—pages 171 and 173

    Puzzle Pieces—pages 175 and 177

2. Place the sorting mats and envelopes of puzzle pieces in the right-hand pocket of the folder.

3. Reproduce a supply of the activity sheet on page 166. Place copies in the left-hand pocket of the folder.

Using the Center

1. The student selects one set of puzzle pieces, the matching sorting mat, and an activity sheet.

2. The student studies the map in the upper-left corner and then places the puzzle pieces in the correct locations to copy the map. The number on the back of each puzzle piece matches the number on the sorting mat. The student follows the same directions to complete the other sorting mat.

3. Next, the student completes the activity sheet by making a map of his or her own classroom.

4. There is no answer key for the activity sheet as the drawings will vary according to the placement of items in the student's own classroom.

Make a Map

Make a map of your classroom.

Make a Map

Make a Map

Follow these steps:

1. Take one set of puzzle pieces and its mat.

2. Put the pieces in the correct places on the mat.

   Use the map at the top of the page to see if you were right.

3. Do the other set the same way.

4. Make a map of your classroom.

Our Classroom

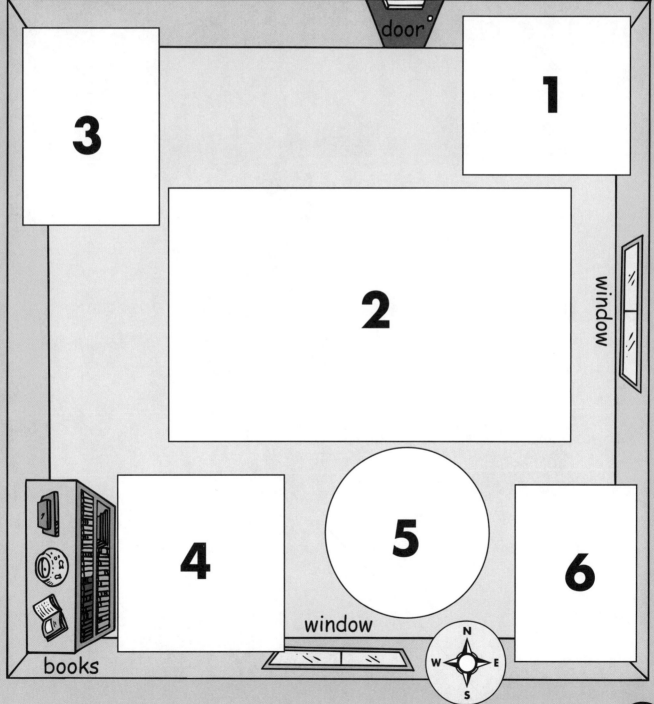

Set 1
Make a Map

©2005 by Evan-Moor Corp. • EMC 3716

Our Town

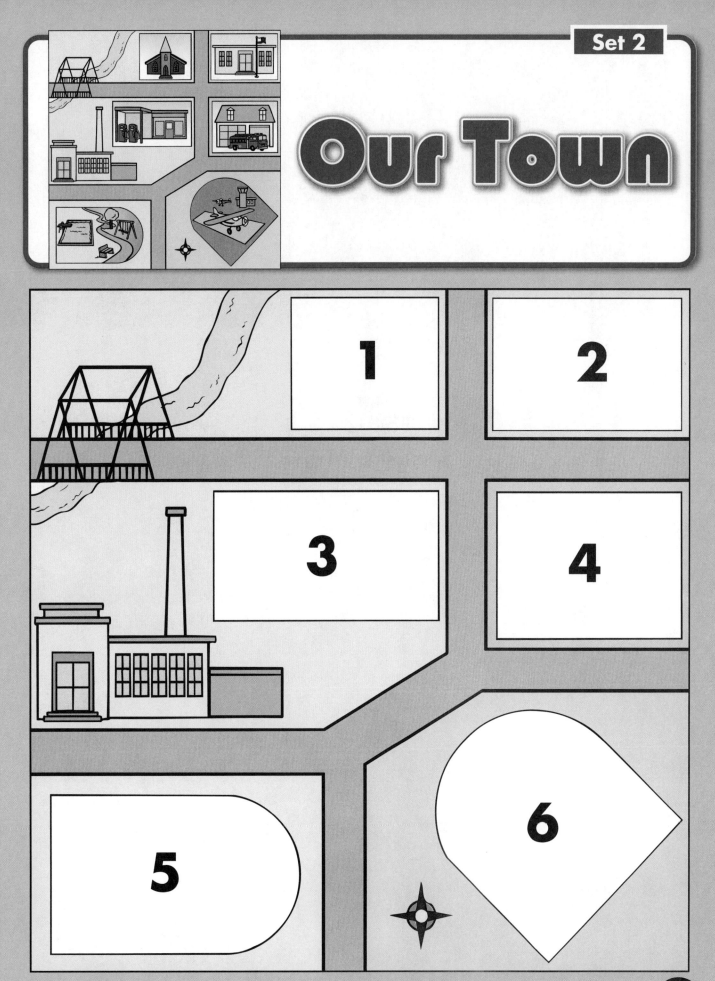

Set 2
Make a Map
©2005 by Evan-Moor Corp. • EMC 3716

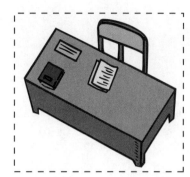

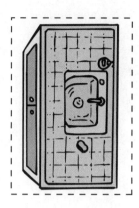

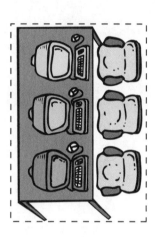

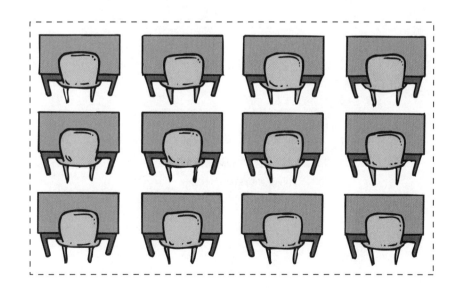

6

Set 1

Our Classroom

©2005 by Evan-Moor Corp.
EMC 3716

1

Set 1

Our Classroom

©2005 by Evan-Moor Corp.
EMC 3716

4

Set 1

Our Classroom

©2005 by Evan-Moor Corp.
EMC 3716

3

Set 1

Our Classroom

©2005 by Evan-Moor Corp.
EMC 3716

5

Set 1

Our Classroom

©2005 by Evan-Moor Corp.
EMC 3716

2

Set 1

Our Classroom

©2005 by Evan-Moor Corp.
EMC 3716

6

Set 2
Our Town
©2005 by Evan-Moor Corp.
EMC 3716

1

Set 2
Our Town
©2005 by Evan-Moor Corp.
EMC 3716

4

Set 2
Our Town
©2005 by Evan-Moor Corp.
EMC 3716

2

Set 2
Our Town
©2005 by Evan-Moor Corp.
EMC 3716

3

Set 2
Our Town
©2005 by Evan-Moor Corp.
EMC 3716

5

Set 2
Our Town
©2005 by Evan-Moor Corp.
EMC 3716

Read a Map

Maps and Activity Sheet Answer Key

Folder Cover

Student Directions

Preparing the Center

1. Prepare a folder following the directions on page 3.

    Cover—page 181

    Student Directions—page 183

    Maps—pages 185–189

    Activity Sheet Answer Key—page 191

2. Laminate the maps and place them in the right-hand pocket of the folder.

3. Reproduce a supply of the activity sheet on page 180. Place copies in the left-hand pocket of the folder.

Using the Center

1. The student takes the three maps and an activity sheet.

2. Using Map A, the student studies the map, reads one question at a time on the activity sheet, and writes the answer.

3. Next, the student follows the same directions using Map B and Map C.

4. The student uses the activity sheet answer key to check his or her answers.

Read a Map

Look at each map. Then write the answers on the lines.

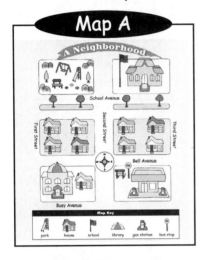

1. What is the **title** of the map?

_____

2. What does 🚩 stand for?

_____

3. What is west of the school?

_____

1. What is the **title** of the map?

_____

2. What does 🛖 stand for?

_____

3. Are the hills north or south of the river?

_____

1. What is the **title** of the map?

_____

2. Is there a **map key** on this map?

_____

3. Is the sandbox east or west of the table?

_____

Read a Map

Read a Map

Follow these steps:

1. Take Map A and the activity sheet.

2. Look at the map. Read the questions.

3. Write the answers on the activity sheet.

4. Do Maps B and C the same way.

5. When you have completed the activity sheet, check your answers.

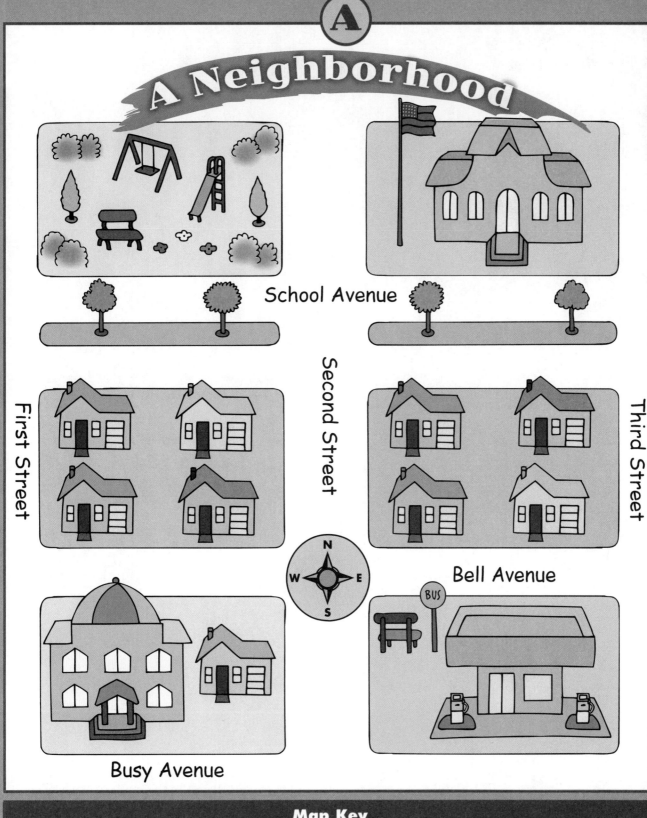

A Neighborhood

School Avenue

First Street

Second Street

Third Street

Bell Avenue

Busy Avenue

Map Key

park house school library gas station bus stop

Read a Map

©2005 by Evan-Moor Corp. • EMC 3716

Read a Map

©2005 by Evan-Moor Corp. • EMC 3716

THE BACKYARD

Read a Map

©2005 by Evan-Moor Corp. • EMC 3716

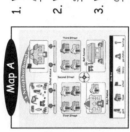

Map A

1. What is the title of the map?
   A Neighborhood

2. What does 🏫 stand for?
   school

3. What is west of the school?
   a park

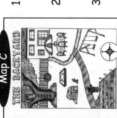

Map B

1. What is the title of the map?
   Nature Park

2. What does 🏕 stand for?
   picnic area

3. Are the hills north or south of the river?
   north

Map C

1. What is the title of the map?
   The Backyard

2. Is there a map key on this map?
   no

3. Is the sandbox east or west of the table?
   west

Read a Map

Lift the flap to check
your answers.

Read a Map

©2005 by Evan-Moor Corp. • EMC 3716

Read a Map

©2005 by Evan-Moor Corp. • EMC 3716